D0970446

the Zen
of selling

the Zen of selling

of selling

*the Way to profit
from life's everyday lessons*

Stan Adler

AMACOM
American Management Association
New York · Atlanta · Boston · Chicago · Kansas City · San Francisco · Washington, D.C.
Brussels · Mexico City · Tokyo · Toronto

Library of Congress Cataloging-in-Publication Data
Adler, Stan.
    The Zen of selling : the way to profit from life's everyday
lessons / Stan Adler.
      p.   cm.
ISBN 0-8144-0433-2
1. Selling   I. Title.
HF5438.25.A35   1998
658.85--dc21   98-21612
                                                          CIP

Printing number

10   9   8   7   6   5   4   3   2   1

To
Mom and Dad,
who let me do anything I wanted to do,
and Carol, Chris, and Jennifer,
who made sure I did it

There is no Beginning.
And there is no Ending.
Our experience is always
Only an excerpt.
—Richard Stine

Contents

Acknowledgments

To Laurie Harper, my sagacious literary agent, for championing a book that she knew was not just another sales book: Thank you for the know-how, dedication, and support that made the book possible.

To Maggie Stuckey, personal editor and writing guru, who caught the essence of the book with uncanny concision, made sense of stories gone awry, turned thoughts into phrases, found clarity in a thicket of ideas, and showed the genuine care and generous nature that make it all worthwhile. I know you're the best in the business, but, more important, I know you as a friend. Thank you from the bottom of my heart for your encouragement, talent, and patience.

To Mary Glenn for saying yes first; to my publisher, Hank Kennedy, and my editor, Ellen Kadin, and all the other folks at AMACOM who went out of their way to make this one special.

To Jack Adler, my father and teacher, the first writer in the family, who showed me the paths, the rocks, and the reflections in the lake and taught me how to go to the shore and come back again. To Lela, my mother, who taught me how to smile and love life gently when it came my way, who showed me the meaning of kindness, inner strength, and the things I can learn when I listen. To my sister, Joy, who has given me so much of that—thank you for being you.

To Carol, my wife, who sponsored my dreams, patiently nurtured a career and, quite literally, my life, and who will never know how important and beautiful a partner she is and always will be. To Chris, my daughter, who repairs my dreams when they are snared by the bright light of day— who gave me a working title as if it were a step to a place I must go. To Jennifer, my daughter, who gives me sage advice and understanding of things about which I have never asked but have always needed to know—I will use it like a bag of magic, with respect and gratitude. To the three of you, dear ones, together and apart, thank you for your love.

To Lawton and Val, Nan, Steve Wiley, Steve Fulk, Bill and Sally, Jeff and Bonnie, Ron and Patti, John Bolton, Patrick Robertson, Bill Meyer, Rick and Dede, George and Ann, and Morgan Mayfield for your support and encouragement.

To all the salespeople who said thank you.

To my teachers and mentors during the early course of things: Irving Halperin, Hansje, Ted Bennett, Steve Satterlee (where *do* we go one subliminal step at a time?), David Smith, Marvin Crowson, and Don Vernine.

And, finally, in memory of Kay Meyers, a dear friend.

꧁ Introduction ꧂

I'd like to begin by introducing you to my friend Victor, who plays a prominent role in this book.

Victor has never owned a business or been a CEO, yet he has served on the board of half a dozen Fortune 500 companies and been responsible for spending, exchanging, and investing millions of dollars. He has served as adviser and consultant to world business and political leaders, set diplomatic precedents, expedited trade agreements, and championed ecology as a corporate issue. He has been on the front pages of the world's foremost news publications several times.

In the course of his travels and accomplishments, Victor has acquired refined and exotic tastes. If Victor drives it, drinks it, or reads it, it's probably worthy of your respect. He's a bit older than I, but there's something ageless, timeless about him. He is the smartest person I know, and the wisest.

Victor has always had a fascination—some call it an obsession—with the selling of things, tangible and intangible, and the managing of people, all kinds of people. I feel fortunate to have him as a friend, yet he has the grace to make me feel like the host of our friendship. This is a hallmark of the master seller and communicator that he is. His ability to remain open to new experiences, disclose fresh insights, and share his all-inclusive love of life is his greatest enjoyment.

When my daughter was in her teens, she once described Victor as a "formal kind of wise man."

I agreed, but added somewhat defensively, "But Victor isn't stuffy."

"Oh, no!" she replied. "Victor is cool."

Victor laughed at her description of him, but he clearly liked it. I wish to convey my special thanks to Victor—a "cool, formal kind of wise man"—for guiding me over the years, for taking the time to be such an integral part of this book.

ᛏ   ᛏ

Victor has an ability to untangle complex issues and see through to the essence. I fondly recall a phone conversation during which I told Victor about the sales seminar I had just finished giving. I think I was expounding rather grandly about radically modifying sales archetypes and finding a way to communicate the sales process more directly.

At an appropriate moment in the conversation, Victor said, "Stan, do you know what you really do in your seminars? Help people get along. It's all a matter of understanding—*immediately*. It's sort of like the Zen of selling."

I have spent more than twenty years—most of my professional life—teaching salespeople how to sell. Through those years, I have scrutinized literally hundreds of books on sales techniques and have examined all the trendy and overcomplicated theories, concepts, systems, matrices, quadrants, grids, and other paradigms that have been used to explain, and sometimes confuse, the act of selling.

I have also, for the better part of my life, enjoyed a sometimes studious, often casual, but always fulfilling relationship with something called Zen.

So Victor's offhand comment about the Zen of selling

created in me one of those thrilling "clicks" when two ideas come together in a new way. It is, I have often thought, Victor's special gift to trigger those clicks in others. In any event, what Victor said started me thinking about selling, and especially teaching others about selling, in a brand-new way.

Learning how to sell is similar to learning other skills that can be refined as an art. I'm referring to universal skills such as singing, dancing, drawing, writing, playing sports or music, or doing something as personal as making love or being a parent. All of these aspects of life have been addressed by how-to books in a step-by-step, structured fashion, but without much real success.

People do not fare well at being *told* how to play tennis, paint portraits, sell houses, or do anything else that is a mixture of kinetic, emotional, and intellectual energy. People excel in these things only after *seeing, understanding,* and *doing.* And when they do so, they have experienced the Zen of it.

Much of what I know about selling I learned from Victor. So, with my new perception of selling, I decided to document some of Victor's experiences in exactly the same way he shared them with me—in the form of simple stories—within the covers of a book that would *show* rather than *tell* people how to sell. Along the way, I remembered some of my own experiences whose real meaning Victor helped me see and decided they fit into the book as well.

The Zen of selling is exactly seventeen stories long, and within each story you will find an object lesson of an essential step in selling.

My goal is to show a way of selling based purely on understanding customers as people. This, of course, runs counter to most sales literature, which presents adversarial sales strategies where people are a means to an end. I want to show and share insights on what *really* happens when salespeople put themselves, their products, and their customers on the same level of acceptance and act without a single glint of pretension.

For years, it has been my objective to teach salespeople how to make more sales, not only with less effort but also with a greater sense of fulfillment, personally as well as professionally. That is also the objective of this book.

The Zen of selling includes more than making a living. When you accept your role as an important person in the lives of your customers, you make customers feel as special as they individually are. When they feel special, you will feel even more so and will reflect that satisfaction and learn how to profit more from life's everyday experiences.

Zen is neither religion nor philosophy but insight. It is a way of understanding yourself in relation to everything else and discovering something so evident that there is no need to doubt the truth of what you know. It is also a way to distinguish the genuine from the artificial, a way to laugh, express the surprise of your life, and see the game in any plan.

The Zen of selling is a way for you to see and understand the truth of what you do as you sell. It will allow you time to stop and relate and to understand how you can sell better—*today!*

After reading this book, you find out that the secret of selling is no secret at all. It is simply you appreciating and getting to know the people who will, in turn, show their appreciation by buying what you have to sell.

You will immediately sell better because you will immediately have a better understanding of what you do. This improvement may almost seem miraculous; it is the miracle of you saying, "Yes, I can do it."

The Zen of selling is a *yes* in a world of too many noes.

Stan Adler

❧ 1 ❧

Opportunity of a Lifetime Revisited

You know your customer. You know how he works and how he thinks, how organized or disorganized he is, whether he listens most of the time or does most of the talking. You know your product and know what gets the applause and what doesn't. You know when to be thorough and when to overview.

You know how to say hello, exchange pleasantries. You know enough about your customer to ask about his vacation or his kids or wish him happy birthday. And if you don't know these things, you'll ask the right questions and learn enough in the first few minutes of your meeting to create the illusion that you're an old acquaintance.

You know how to segue from small talk to the important issues. You know when to stop the selling and let the buying begin. You're prepared, confident, and focused. You're feeling bright and cheerful and can't wait to greet your customer. You have everything in order. What could possibly go wrong?

Well, the customer may have forgotten the appointment even though you confirmed it yesterday. Or perhaps something totally unexpected came up, and he didn't have time to phone before you left the office. Maybe he decided to take a position with another company, but that's crazy thinking, and expecting the worst is not the way to do your best.

Instead, visualize it all happening the way it should happen. *Affirm*, it will happen like it's supposed to happen, unless the customer just doesn't like you, but even that's not a problem if the customer likes what you're selling. It's just a matter of shifting focus. Take responsibility for your own actions, for those things you can control, and for your reactions to those things you cannot control.

Sometimes even the most talented and sensitive sellers are not prepared for what's around the corner.

ዮ   ዒ

Victor is famous for regaling people at dinner parties with stories of financial intrigue featuring well-known names, but my favorite story is one that I've never heard him tell anyone other than me.

It took place early in Victor's career, when he was a young, ambitious bank officer. His job was to sell his bank's services to companies who already had comfortable banking relationships. His challenge, he said, was similar to that of any other salesperson. He was like the Fuller Brush man selling brushes to people who already had a closet full of brushes.

The bank that he represented had some noteworthy advantages over other competitive financial organizations. He was a master at describing the benefits of these advantages so that they appeared to be singularly unique services.

Maybe he was just selling another brush, but it was his ability to present a brush especially created for a prescribed task that made it so irresistibly salable.

This particular day he had an appointment with the treasurer of a major *Fortune* 500 corporation. He understood the importance of the occasion and was properly prepared. He sensed the challenge but was not in awe.

He arrived early enough to give himself time to arrange his presentation materials and to make a final inspection of his personal appearance, but he was careful not to be *too* early. He did not want to feel as if he were being kept waiting, for he knew that could create a negative frame of mind. He had thoroughly researched the company's background and felt no need to review his notes again. A credible presentation relied heavily on the moment at hand. That spark of spontaneity and sensitivity to the immediacy of your surroundings was something you could not fake. As Victor put it: "If you enjoy what you do, it is wonderfully evident."

A receptionist escorted him past the first reception area and introduced him to a secretary, who, in turn, introduced him to the treasurer's assistant, who assured him that it would just be a few moments.

Soon he was ushered into the treasurer's office. Although the well-appointed office allowed for ample casual seating, the treasurer, Mr. Brubaker, remained seated at his desk. The desk was slightly elevated. A less trained eye would not have noticed it.

Mr. Brubaker motioned Victor to have a seat in one of the plush chairs in front of the desk. He chose the one on the right. Years ago, he had been told to sit to the right of a person whom you faced at a first meeting. The position to the left of the person was reserved for trusted advisers—a role that Victor always envisioned himself filling at a later date, but not quite yet.

Victor presented his card by way of introduction and sat back in the chair. The shape of the chair discouraged an active posture, but he tolerated its embrace rather than perching on the edge of the chair. An edge-of-the-seat posture invoked images of serfs begging for a landowner's favors or seals barking for fish.

A few minutes of casual conversation ensued, just enough time to get a feeling for Brubaker's role in the company; then, just as Victor was ready to describe his main competitive edge, Brubaker looked at his watch. With his right hand he was impatiently tapping Victor's card against the desk.

"Young man," he said, interrupting Victor in mid-sentence, "what can you give me that I can't get from my existing banks?"

Victor nodded and smiled, signifying that he not only understood the question but welcomed it. The question could not have come at a better time. It acted as a segue to his next statement.

"Mr. Brubaker, since you are conversant with services that are offered with a sense of personal . . . um . . . "

As he looked across the desk at Brubaker, the normally articulate Victor began to stammer. He couldn't believe what he was seeing. The man was slowly, methodically tearing Victor's business card into small strips and depositing them, one by one, into a clean crystal ashtray.

When the treasurer finished shredding the card, he stood up, thanked Victor for his time, and announced he was late for another appointment.

Thoroughly flustered, Victor was relieved to leave the office. At the door, he glanced back at the remnants of his card in the ashtray. It was a kind of effigy.

Victor had another appointment later that afternoon. He knew he needed to collect himself for that meeting, so he stopped in the men's room in Brubaker's building. He splashed cool water on his face and took a good look at himself in the mirror. He was shocked at his own appearance. He did not look prepared; he looked devastated. He knew he was in no condition to make another presentation.

Using a pay phone in the lobby, Victor attempted to reschedule his next appointment. It was not possible to reschedule, so he felt he had no choice but to cancel. It was the first time in his career he had ever done that. It was also the last.

ၜ   ၛ

When he finished telling me the story, Victor asked for one of my business cards. I took one from my card case and handed it to him. "Stan, all he did was this. . . . "

I didn't believe Victor was actually going to do it, and I didn't realize the true nature of what he had described until, as casually as if he were opening an envelope, he tore up my business card.

I watched with the same sense of disbelief that must have been his, years before. He had destroyed today's calling card and tomorrow's reference. The present and future of a professional salesperson.

"They tell you all your life not to take it personally," he said, "but every time *it* comes around we usually respond to it in our own inimitable and personal ways. Sometimes we blame, or rationalize, or overanalyze, or just plain sulk. And that's the point, which it's taken me a number of years to understand. It's not what happens to you that knocks you out—it's your response. In other words, how you feel when you fail is up to you. And that is something that you can control."

"But Victor, that was a terrible thing that happened. Anyone would have been upset."

"Of course it was. But I allowed it to become more important than it need have been. It's too easy to fall on your own sword or wallow in the puddle that you're standing in. Self-pity excuses your worst behavior without pointing the way to a better place. And you can't afford to let an exception depreciate your value or take you off course."

While he talked, Victor was absentmindedly reassembling the pieces of my card. "Understanding is not just for other people, my friend, but for yourself as well. Take time to understand what went awry and how you can make it right should it ever occur again. Forgive yourself; then move on swiftly. If it's an irreconcilable situation, as with Brubaker, at least have the good sense to keep your next appointment. Stan, I had plenty of cards, but who knows, by canceling that meeting, I may have canceled the opportunity of a lifetime."

That's the definition of business; something goes through, something else doesn't. Make use of one, forget the other.

— Henry Becque

❧ 2 ❧

How to Fix a Customer

Selling is customer service, and customer service is selling. The two actions are indistinguishable parts of a seamless process.

Salespeople who make a distinction between the two tend to subscribe to the old scenario, in which "selling" means get the sale and forget the customer, and "customer service" means do as little as possible to quick-fix any problems that crop up. They see selling as something that you do *to* someone, and customer service as something you do *for* someone, albeit reluctantly.

It is your job to make the customer feel better about buying, to make the buying process a reasonable, intelligent, and enjoyable exchange. Whether your customer is a senior citizen counting out change at the grocery checkstand or a world leader trading commodity futures for high technology, your role is to answer concerns, balance priorities, work out potential problems, clarify confusion, solve unavoidable conflicts, and maintain equanimity even if the situation becomes volatile. You must never lose sight of the fact that you are working for—not against—the customer.

When making the sale becomes a goal unto itself and the customer is considered a necessary evil, inevitably there are hurt feelings and disappointment. But when customer service is your primary objective during and after the sale, things tend to go right. The customer feels right, feels good about buying, and looks forward to doing business with you again.

ঁ   ঁ

Several years ago, the month of January brought record low temperatures to the fair-weather state of California. Temperatures dropped into the teens, and water pipes all over town began bursting.

I was watching the local news, feeling smug and a little bit guilty that we had escaped the problem, when I heard a loud snap and the sickening sound of rushing water. An outside pipe had split open, and a torrent of water was blasting onto the basement window. I yanked the bottom segment off the downspout and used it to divert the flow away from the house.

It was a temporary solution, but not a bad one, and I was feeling rather proud of myself as I started calling plumbers to arrange for a professional repair.

I soon found out I was low priority. Six different plumbers told me they had customers who had no water at all, and they didn't know when they could get to me. So then I tried calling hardware stores for advice on how to repair a copper pipe. Responses were curt. One clerk told me he had twelve people at the counter, all demanding supplies he no longer had. With each call, my questions and my temper got shorter.

The people I talked to were demonstrating a free-market truth: When demand for goods and service exceeds supply, courtesy is often the first casualty. I myself was demonstrating another: Expect the worst and adopt a nasty attitude, and you'll get just what you expect.

An hour and many phone calls later, I finally located a hardware store in a town twenty miles away that still had two half-inch pipe clamps. "If you can get here within the hour," the owner said, "I'll save one of them for you."

So I grabbed a jacket and raced out. Thirty minutes later I dashed into the store. A very young woman—a girl, really—was behind the counter.

"I'm the guy who called about the clamp," I said, slightly out of breath. She frowned, looked at me with a puzzled expression, and then searched through several boxes behind the counter. Nothing.

"Let me see if I can find my dad. Maybe he'll know."

Her father, the owner, was helping two other customers in the rear of the store, but he told her to look in the box under the counter.

"But I already looked there, Dad. It's not there."

"Look again. I know I put it there."

The tension was starting to get to them. Their voices got louder, and everyone in the store could hear. My own frustration was rising by the minute.

As the young woman returned to the front counter, an older woman—obviously her mother—came up from another part of the store and asked what was going on. With a pained expression on her face, she turned to me. "I'm so sorry, I sold those about five minutes ago. I didn't know he was saving them."

And at that moment I lost it. "Damn it! I drove all the way over here for something you don't even have? What kind of place are you running here?"

Now the owner joined us at the front counter. He quickly realized the situation and tried his best to apologize. "I understand how you must feel," he said softly. "I'm terribly sorry. If you have a minute, I think I can find something else that might work."

But I was having none of it. Furious, I turned and stomped out, slamming the door harder than I meant to. The bell on the door clattered against the glass.

A mile away, I stood shivering in an open phone booth, staring blindly at the Yellow Pages and calling myself stupid. Stupid for trying to find something that wasn't available and for trying to make another person feel as frustrated as I was because of an unintentional mistake. I had allowed myself to take the mistake personally, and I had managed to insult the whole family—husband, wife, and daughter.

I drove back to the store. Both women were behind the counter. I smiled sheepishly and asked if I could speak to the man.

"I just wanted to tell you that I'm sorry for acting the way I did," I said when he came up to the counter. "And I apologize to both of you"—to the two women—"for losing my temper. That was uncalled for." They both smiled, and the daughter blushed.

I'll never forget the father's response. With a kind smile, he said, "That's okay. If you can't understand your customer's frustrations, you don't deserve to be in business." We shook hands, grinning. "Now," he said, "let's see if we can get you fixed up."

The man knew his hardware. In a very short time, I left the store with a two-dollar part, and two hours later the leak was fixed. He also knows his business: My dignity as a person and as a customer had been restored, along with my disposition.

Now, whenever I need something from a hardware store, I drive twenty miles out of my way, and I do it with a smile.

ꢳ   ꢡ

Not long after this, Victor and I were strolling in the wooded area just below my house. A few minutes earlier, as we headed down toward the woods, he had spotted the bright new copper pipe and had asked about it. Now, as we walked along, I told him the story. Victor had picked up a Douglas fir cone and was idly tossing it from one hand to the other as he listened.

I would bet even money that Victor has never been in a hardware store in his life, but he instantly understood why the hardware merchant's behavior had affected me so strongly. "Empathy," he said. "That's what made the difference. Your friend is a true seller. He instinctively knows that his job is to show understanding even when the customer doesn't deserve it. And that's the essence of service.

"The truth is, Stan," he continued, his voice dropping almost to a whisper, as if to share a secret, "you can't remove customer service from the act of selling. It's *all* service. It's like this cone. If I decide to remove the scales from the cone, in short order I have no cone at all. The scales *are* the cone; they're inseparable."

As he talked, Victor had been pulling off the scales and dropping them on the path. "Here," he said, handing me the bare spike. *"Pseudotsuga*, Latin for "false hemlock." We call it Douglas fir. But botanically it's neither a hemlock nor a fir. Magnificent tree, even if we humans are confused about what to call it."

Fix the customer.

Then fix the pipe.

—*Victor*

ᖆ 3 ᖅ

The Close Is Like a Compass

Most of the how-to sales books and instruction manuals that talk about closings are presumptuous, bordering on preposterous. Every day, millions of salespeople are sternly advised to "get the order" and to "ask for the sale." They are conditioned to believe that customers buy because they are asked to.

This fixation on closing can blind you to what you must do before getting to that point. There is a way to move and a manner of communicating that make it inevitable you will achieve your objective—and then a programmed close is irrelevant. Selling is significant conversation, keen awareness, perceptions and understanding, timing and balance, pacing and positioning: a simple but subtle matter of cause and effect. You listen when the other person speaks. You move forward when the other person moves backward. Skillful selling is like dancing, but compulsive closers turn it into a wrestling match.

People don't buy because you ask them to; they buy because they feel like it. As a master seller, you must be attuned to the feelings of everyone around you. It is your job

—and your pleasure—to encourage, persuade, convince, clarify, instill desire, and provide both fanciful and sound rationales that are clear, cool, and tempting.

Sometimes customers are very close to the buying decision, and sometimes they are very distant. You must at all times be keenly aware of your position relative to the customer's. You must be able to connect emotionally with the customers at their level. You must know when to make your next move so that it complements the customer's (remember the dance). Often this is a matter more of intuition than of conscious planning.

What you must not do is, through panic, resort to a clichéd trial close. Don't ask, "What's your budget?" or "When are you planning on making a decision?" or "What will it take for us to do business?" These are things you should already have found out, but in a more skillful manner.

You are, in the final analysis, your own best resource. You must call upon your own experience and your empathetic understanding. You must trust your perceptions and your ability to quickly decode what you have seen and heard and then respond with an appropriate, attractive move that will allow the customer to move closer to the buying decision.

When your customer looks at you and asks, "What kind of arrangements should I make?" or "What do we have to do next?" then you know you have done your job. It is time to step aside and allow your customers to own what you have sold them and what they have bought. Selling and buying are, after all, just two sides of a mutually satisfying experience.

℘   ℘

One evening late in September, Victor and I were sitting on my patio, drinking iced tea and talking about the special excitement of closing a big sale. I said something about making an emotional connection with the customer, and that reminded him of this story.

"It was early in 1973. One morning I got a call from the State Department." I must have looked surprised, for Victor added, "The Assistant Secretary and I were in college together; we've kept in touch. At any rate, he asked if I could make myself available to take a certain document to Paris and get it signed. The Arabs were threatening an oil embargo, and this was part of a U.S.-European attempt to forestall it."

"But, Victor, why you? Why not send someone from the government?"

"Precisely because I was *not* from the government. This had to be completely sub rosa. Officially, the United States could not be involved in the negotiations. Of course I said yes. It was one of the greatest experiences of my life. I always think of it when people talk about closings. I think you'll see why."

℘   ℘

Victor's assignment was simple: Be at a certain office in a certain government building at 9:00 A.M. Meet with a French representative, go over the document in detail, clarify any questions. Get a signature.

It was not unlike a salesperson who has been given an

account with full assurance that the client is ready to buy. All that remains is getting him to sign on the dotted line. For a master seller like Victor, a simple task indeed.

It didn't work out quite that way.

Victor's counterpart was a career bureaucrat named Foyier, a fit-looking man in his early sixties. His manner was brusque and no-nonsense, and, after the briefest of greetings, they got right to work.

For the next half hour, Foyier went over every paragraph in detail, asking questions like, "Is this inclusive of all parties or only one party?" Victor, who had committed the document to memory and spoke French fluently, was able to resolve all questions to Foyier's satisfaction. With each answer, Foyier became a bit more cordial. Finally, sensing that the moment of signing was near, Victor reached into his pocket for a fountain pen he had intentionally brought along for this important occasion.

It was a Mont Blanc Meisterstück, a rare lapis lazuli model 25. In the past, whenever Victor had used it, people had often commented on its beauty. Now Victor unscrewed the cap, slipped the cap on the bottom of the pen, and handed the pen to Foyier.

Instantly Foyier's manner changed. "Get that pen away from me!" he shouted. "How can you ask me to sign papers of accord with that . . . that SS souvenir? Do you not know how many French men and women died at the hands of the SS? Do you know that I was a member of the Resistance? I will not touch that pen." He pushed away from the desk, crossed his arms defiantly, and glared at Victor.

Victor was stunned. For a moment he couldn't imagine

what Foyier was talking about. And then he remembered an old rumor that Hitler had commissioned the Mont Blanc corporation to make pens for his top SS officers. It was in all likelihood an apocryphal story—after all, Mont Blanc had been making pens since the beginning of the twentieth century—but at that moment the entire negotiation depended on it.

Simply setting the record straight about the facts wouldn't be sufficient, Victor realized. Foyier's emotions were too high. His only hope was to respond with something that would have an equally strong emotional impact but would defuse the anger. Then suddenly Victor remembered something.

"Monsieur," Victor said quietly to Foyier, "my apologies for causing you distress. I believe that I understand. My pen is a Mont Blanc. A German pen with a French name. I am familiar with the event you refer to, but did you know that there is more to the story? I have heard that the penmaker who designed the pen at Hitler's order was Jewish. He found a way to strike back."

Victor held the pen upright and touched the cap. "This symbol here . . . most people assume it represents Mont Blanc, the mountain. If you look at the pen from the side, it certainly appears to be a mountain in silhouette. But if you look at it from the top, you can see something else. It is actually the designer's rendition of the Star of David."

Victor tipped the pen slightly toward Foyier, giving him a bird's-eye view of the cap. "What you see here may have been one of the most powerful underground statements made during the war. A beautiful, elegant act of resistance."

Foyier sat perfectly still for what seemed like a long time. Then slowly his expression changed. As Victor watched, his face gradually relaxed, starting at his eyebrows, then his eyes, then his mouth and chin. He still didn't speak but reached out his hand for the pen and signed the paper with a great Gallic flourish. Then he came over to Victor's side of the desk and embraced him joyously, kissing Victor on both cheeks.

At the end of his story, Victor remained quiet for a time. When he continued, his voice was soft. "Well, as you know, we had the oil embargo anyway. So I suppose in that sense we failed. But as I left that room that day, I felt like a grand success. I've closed many sales, but none that was more important, or more fulfilling."

I cleared my throat. "Victor, is that story true?"

"You mean the part about Hitler?"

"And the Jewish pen maker."

"I'm not sure. That rumor has been going around Europe since the end of World War II. The person who told it to me thought it was true. But that's not really the point, is it?"

Victor and I share an appreciation of fine implements. Many years ago, shortly after we first met, he showed me one of his prized possessions: an old military lensatic compass. As Victor carefully removed the compass from its leather case, he said to me, "This is as close as you'll ever get to a good close."

I was young and cocky then, and I thought I knew all there was to know about closing a sale. I started to object to this esoteric comparison, but Victor continued. "A close is like a compass—you only need it when you're lost, or in danger of getting off the track. If your customers seem to lose interest, if you have no real idea where they are or where you are, if things drag on with endless repetition of the same concerns and you have no clear indication of the customer's true feelings, that's when you need to take a bearing. That's the time for a closing action, and that's the only time. Otherwise, remember your job is to show the customer a way to buy with satisfaction. Forget the selling. Let the customer do the buying."

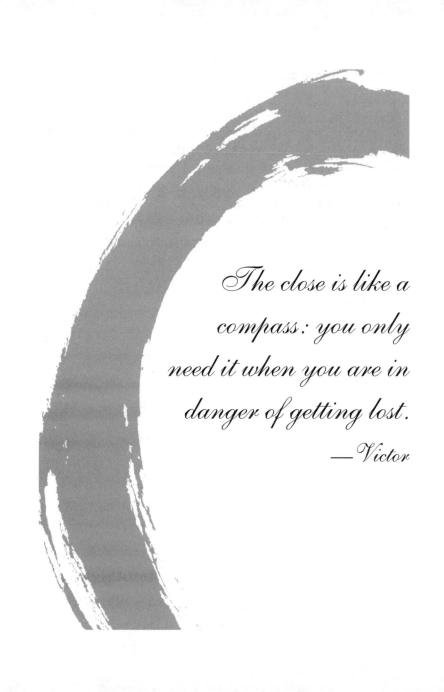

The close is like a compass: you only need it when you are in danger of getting lost.

—Victor

❧ 4 ❧

It's Not a Question of Price

"**H**ow much do you want to spend?"

That is the absolute worst thing you can say to a customer, and yet salespeople do it all the time with no sense of how grave an error it is. No matter what the product, from personal computers to personal retirement plans, this is the wrong question. No matter who your customers are or how much they may or may not already know about the product, this is *always* a mistake.

If customers don't know how much they want to spend, which is the case if they haven't purchased this product recently or done their homework, they have no idea how to answer the question. And that makes them very uncomfortable. The only thing you have achieved is to create a negative atmosphere. People invariably feel intimidated and defensive. No one wants to admit to ignorance, so their immediate reaction is to find an excuse to get away as quickly as possible. Or they have the vague suspicion that you're trying to put something over on them, with the same result: a desire to escape as fast as they can.

Even if customers *do* know what they want to spend, asking this question is a serious mistake. In fact, it is usually an even bigger mistake in this circumstance. Introducing the issue of price achieves only one thing: It calls customers' attention to the price. And make no bones about it, they can find your product somewhere else at the same price, even a better price, in a snap. By getting customers to focus on price, you have given them a wonderful reason to walk away. You have turned the process on its head.

Your focus instead should be on the qualities of the product itself, and on you as the representative. Your goal is to use the product as a way to show your value to customers so that they will want to buy from you rather than from someone else. If you do your job properly, customers will come to think of you as indispensable. Not only will they gladly buy this particular product from you; they will want to do business with you again and again. It's the difference between a long-term business relationship and a one-shot sale. It's the difference between a one-invoice mentality and the style of a true professional.

A few years ago my daughter and I set out on a Saturday morning to buy her a new bike. She had outgrown her old one, and this was to be our present for her tenth birthday. We started at a bike shop near our home.

I remember Tracy pausing just inside the door of the shop, momentarily awed by the rows and rows of bikes. Then she spotted the one she liked and marched over to it with me in tow. As she stood with her left hand on the seat of the shiny red bicycle, a salesperson approached.

It had been a while since I shopped for a bike, and I tried to think of the right questions to ask.

"She seems to like this one. Is this a good choice for her?"

"It's a really good bicycle," he answered, looking over our shoulders at another customer coming through the front door.

"Well, what makes it good for us?"

"It's very popular; we sell a lot of 'em."

"But I'm wondering if it has the right features for my daughter."

"Well, how much did you want to spend?"

Tracy stepped back from the bicycle. I started to say something, then stopped. This wasn't making sense. "Actually," I said, "we're just looking today; maybe we'll come back later."

The salesperson shrugged. "Okay. I'll be here when you're ready."

And, over Tracy's protests, we left.

Later that afternoon, we bought the same bicycle at another shop not fifteen minutes away. It was the very same model, probably the same price, but there was one big difference: Paul.

When we entered the second shop, Tracy spied her bicycle and headed toward it. A smiling salesperson came over, introduced himself as Paul, and shook hands with both of us.

"I can tell you really like this one, Tracy," he said. "What do you like about it?"

"I like the color. Red is my favorite color. And I like the name. One of my friends has this same bike, but not red."

"Where do you think you'll be riding it?"

"Around," she answered, running one finger across the smooth anodized handlebars. "Maybe to school sometimes."

"How far is that?" Paul asked.

"It's not too far. Just a few blocks."

Without shifting his attention from Tracy, Paul quickly looked up at me and nodded understanding when I held up seven fingers.

"And do you ride on the street to get to school or on the sidewalk?"

"On the sidewalk. Except when I cross the street, of course," she said seriously.

"Of course." Paul didn't smile. Neither did I. "What kind of bicycle do you have now, Tracy?"

"A four-speed," she answered. "We're going to give it to my sister. It's still a good bike."

"Great! That's how I got my first bike, too—from my big sister. Tell me something—did it take you long to learn to use the gears?"

We stayed there for the better part of an hour. Paul continued his friendly conversation with Tracy, drawing out from her information about how she would be using the new bike, what she liked and didn't like about her old one. She never stepped back from the red bicycle.

"How about you sit on the seat, Tracy," Paul suggested, "and let's see how this one fits."

The seat was too high. While he chatted with Tracy about his own experience with a bike just like this, Paul quickly adjusted the seat to her height and asked her to hop up again. She put both hands on the handlebars and moved one of the gear levers. Paul began explaining which levers moved which gears and showed her the correct gear combinations for most riding situations.

"I don't think I can remember all that," she said, frowning.

"Okay, I'll write it down for you."

And he did. He pulled out a small notebook from his back pocket and made a list of the main points. He also went over the correct braking procedure and some safety tips.

"And if you forget any of this," he added, handing her a business card, "you can call me any time. Here's my number."

I'm sure my daughter had never had anyone give her a business card before. She held it carefully, with both hands, as we drove away.

In the car, along with a proud papa and a beaming ten-year-old girl, were one brand-new bike, a new helmet, and a tool bag with the name of the shop on it.

Since then, I have referred several people to that shop. Last summer I bought a new bike for myself and had the opportunity to watch a repeat performance as Paul skillfully moved me from shopper to excited buyer.

And he never once asked me, "How much do you want to spend?"

ᕈ ᕀ

At Tracy's birthday party a few days later, I told Victor about this experience. I found myself struggling to explain the difference between these two very different salespeople. "It's not just that one was nice and one was sort of a jerk.

There was something much more basic there, and it's not about bicycles at all. Could be about anything."

Victor smiled that little smile he gets when I've said something important but don't realize it. And then he invited me to try a simple exercise. Like most of Victor's "simple" exercises, this one is about something profound, and I've never forgotten it.

"Stan, think of something that you would like to own but have never sold professionally. Stocks, for instance, or a sailboat, or a new car—"

"Minivan," I interrupted. We had been looking for a vehicle with more room for the kids, their friends, and a couple of bikes.

"Good. Now think of four or five things about a minivan that would be important to you, other than price." He turned his Happy Birthday napkin over to the clean side. "Write them down."

In just a few seconds I scribbled:

Safety features?
Repair history?
Gas mileage?
Resale value?
Storage capacity?

And pushed the napkin back to Victor.

"Now then," he said. "Would the answers to those questions affect your feeling about the price of a particular model?"

"Of course," I blurted. "Any one . . ." And then, as the full impact of his lesson hit me, I paused.

Victor's gentle smile came back. "The product, you see, justifies the price—not the other way around."

Don't spend precious time negotiating the price of something you haven't sold.

—*Victor*

❧ 5 ❧

How to Make
Chicken Salad Special

We were all waiting impatiently to get off the airplane, and I found myself in that scrunched-up position that is the fate of passengers who have a window seat. The woman in front of me reached up to take her bag down from the overhead compartment, and her beautiful watch caught my eye. It was rectangular, with an ivory face and gold Roman numerals and a caiman leather strap. Very simple, very elegant. I wanted to comment on it, but something held me back. Instead, I continued to stare at the back of passengers' heads and wait for the plane doors to open.

Later on, I regretted not speaking up. That was exactly the watch I would like to have bought Carrie for her birthday, but I knew nothing about it except approximately what it looked like. Had I taken a moment to confirm her good taste, it would have helped both of us to feel better during that slow exit process.

Compliments feel good to get and to give. They take only a few seconds to deliver but may last a lifetime. A friend might have told you that you had a great smile, right after you had got your very *noir* glare down pat. Guess what? You're still looking in the mirror admiring that great smile. Or a fellow traveler may have casually commented on what a great book you were reading, and when that book comes to mind, you know there's more than one person in this world who thinks it's a great book.

You may be giving a presentation to a customer who is wearing an exquisite outfit. The reason she's wearing it is to look good, and a compliment will tell her that she succeeded. Don't wait until the right time; say it when you mean it. Compliments usually sound good anytime you get them or give them.

And since you're already in the business of selling people things that should make their lives better, don't keep compliments to yourself. Talk about a good thing when you notice it. A sincere compliment is a gift from you to another human being, and one that everyone appreciates.

℘   ९

Victor and I were having dinner in a fancy restaurant, and Victor had brought along a '74 Keenan Chardonnay. He handed it to the waiter to open. With one eyebrow raised, the waiter turned the bottle in his hand and studied the label as if he were about to crack a secret code. "It's a beautiful wine," he murmured. "I just hope it hasn't oxidized." He paused, as if that were something that Victor hadn't considered.

"I have this just in case," Victor said, putting a younger but equally rare Chardonnay on the table. The waiter nodded curtly and got on with the business of opening the wine. Victor tasted it; the fruit and acidity were still standing.

Victor usually invited the waiter to taste one of his wines, but not this time. After the waiter had left the table, he said, "That man could take a lesson from the young lady in the delicatessen where I was the other day."

"Victor, I have a hard time picturing you in a deli."

"Nonsense, Stan, I love them. This place is just a couple of doors down from J. Debs, the wine merchant, and the window display was thoroughly delightful, so I went in.

"The place is bigger than it appears from the outside, or perhaps it's the vast array of food that they manage to pack into such a small area. It was near lunchtime, and the place was packed. One of the two counter servers, who seemed to have worked there for quite a long time, had a peculiar way about him. As the next customer in line came up to the counter, he barely paid attention to what the customer said. He seemed to begin preparation before they had completed giving their order. It was as if he knew better than they did what they wanted."

"I know deli countermen like that," I said. "It sort of goes with the territory."

"Well, I deliberately got into the other line. I had intended to pick up some cheese and some pâté for later that evening, but suddenly I realized I was hungry. So, when it was my turn, I tried to order a sandwich, but my mind went completely blank. I couldn't think what I wanted. That ever happen to you?"

"All the time."

"The young woman who was taking care of my line— she couldn't be much over twenty—was marvelous. She sensed my confusion and said, 'Since you like the Asiago, I bet you'd enjoy our chicken salad. We make it fresh here, with capers, mint, and yogurt instead of mayonnaise. Would you like to taste it?' And she gave me a sample from a plastic spoon.

"I was surprised. It was absolutely delicious, and I told her so. She gave me the most charming smile and said, 'Oh, good, I knew you'd like it.' Wasn't that wonderful?"

I've had many conversations with Victor about the business of selling, and I always learn from them, but some are more work than others.

"Victor," I said, "what's so wonderful about chicken salad?"

"No, Stan, not the salad. Her attitude. I didn't know much about what she was selling, not nearly as much as she did, but she thought I had made a good decision. And she told me so."

Suddenly I remembered the daunting experience of buying my first computer, and I understood what Victor was talking about. Too many salespeople work too hard at showing off how much they know. They can't resist playing expert, and invariably they come across as condescending, much as our waiter had. Arrogance, however slight, will always discourage an otherwise healthy relationship.

"I get your point. The woman was genuinely happy that you liked her product and congratulated you for having good taste, while at the same time you were congratulating her for the excellent food. So each of you made the other feel better, and it didn't cost anybody anything."

Victor smiled and picked up his glass. "Have some more of this excellent wine, Stan."

ℊ   ℊ

A couple of weeks later, Victor mentioned that he had called a friend whom he hadn't spoken with in years. When the friend answered, he had started to give his last name to refresh her memory, but she interrupted him. "Victor, how could you ever expect me to forget that magnificent voice?" He said that he smiled all the way through the conversation, his spirits lifted by a spontaneous, sincere compliment.

"She's such a charming person and . . ." Victor's sentence trailed off, and his face took on that look I've seen so often, the look that says he's worked out a new connection.

"Ah Stan, such vanity. She paid *me* a compliment, so I think *she's* charming. But really, that's the point I wanted to make—that complimenting people makes them feel better—and that's also what charm is: making someone else feel better. Too many people work hard at being charming themselves rather than charming others. The essence of charm is *'you are'* rather than *'I am.'*

"When you are doing something for someone else, you are always at your best, whether you are a lawyer, doctor, entertainer, craftsman, or any person seeking to do something worthwhile, and that certainly includes people who sell. That's what makes selling such an inescapably good thing to excel at. That's also what makes chicken salad special."

You know what
charm is: a way of
getting the answer yes
without having asked
any clear question.

—Albert Camus

6

The Invisible Feature

The feature that sells the product is often invisible until the customer notices it. It sometimes takes a customer's viewpoint to point out the efficiency of a particular lever, the convenience of a special service, or the uniqueness of a piece of property.

When the customer spots that favorite feature, he will make a favorable comment, raise an eyebrow, or simply smile. If you are where you should be—fully present, focusing without trying too hard—you will immediately see what your customer sees and will, almost intuitively, understand how the feature fits into the whole idea of what you're selling.

You will respond in the same way you would to a friend who had called your attention to something wonderful that you had missed: with appreciation and acknowledgment that you both like the same details. As a result, the customer will relate to the product *personally* because you understand *her* observations.

It is important to realize that your response is what makes you someone special in the eyes of the customer. By being where the customer is, listening, acknowledging, fully participating in the natural flow of a conversation—in other words, by being yourself with someone else—you are facilitating the flow of a common idea. You are saying, in effect, "I know why you like this and want to do this, and here's how we can do it."

ೕ   ೕ

Victor's friend Jennifer was a high-powered real estate agent, but she expressed her assertiveness in such a way that it was interpreted by clients as "the personal touch." By no coincidence, that was also the slogan on her business card. Jennifer often said the best way to maintain her own personal balance was to hold someone else's hand, the customer's, and guide her through the sales process one step at a time. Making every step count was the challenge.

Jennifer related to her customers so effectively that she often created the feeling of a greater intimacy than actually existed. In fact, it wasn't unusual for customers to get just a little bit jealous when they found out she gave her other customers the same special consideration they had received.

Most of her business was by referral. She opted for no floor time and had other agents handle open houses for her unless the showing was located in a neighborhood that she had staked out as her "farm." She attended the weekly sales meeting but otherwise tried to stay away from the office and all the grousing, ego grooming, and politicking that went on there. For those times when she needed to catch up on paperwork, she had a fully equipped home office.

One evening, she was in that home office installing a new software program when Jeff, a longtime acquaintance, called with a surprising request: "Mom wants to buy a condominium."

Jeff's mother, Deborah, was a very special woman, someone for whom Jennifer had tremendous respect. Now in her late seventies, Deborah had been a very influential person in the days when Hollywood was an entertainment empire without precedent and Los Angeles was becoming a city. She had been friends with two of America's greatest novelists and had advised one of them to return to the South while his genius was still intact; she had dined with the stars —Gable, Grant, and Bergman, to name just a few; and she was a political activist, environmentalist, and woman of letters in her own right. Whenever she attended a social occasion, Deborah would always be surrounded by the most distinguished people at the party.

Deborah currently owned an estate in the wine country, and Jennifer had assumed she intended to stay there forever. But now, Jeff explained, she wanted to move closer to her son and his family. In particular, she had mentioned Tiburon . . . something with an ocean view. But it had to be the perfect place.

Jennifer could think of no other person for whom she would rather find the perfect place. At the same time, she could think of no other person whose standards were higher and no other area where finding the perfect place would be as difficult. It was going to be quite a challenge. Jennifer took a deep breath and calmly assured Jeff she would begin the search immediately.

The next morning, she wasn't surprised to learn there were no bayfront condos available in Tiburon. Getting a Tiburon condominium by the Bay was about as easy as getting a berth at the San Francisco Yacht Club—who knows, something might open up in six or eight years.

All of this meant one thing to Jennifer—don't give up; stay in touch with that exclusive little share of the marketplace. She was determined to deliver on her promise to find the perfect place for the woman she held in such high regard. It would be an opportunity to do something special for some very good friends. It would be like doing a performance with your best friend sitting in the front row, or painting the portrait of someone you had long admired without ever having had the opportunity to tell him so.

Two months later, rather to her amazement, Jennifer found a new listing in Tiburon. The write-up was promising: "Truly one of the best. Upper end unit on the bayside with wonderful light and a superb San Francisco view. . . ." It sounded perfect on paper. Jennifer immediately previewed it, and, to her surprise, it was even better than it had sounded. It met every requirement that Jeff had specified.

She called Jeff and told him the good news. They made arrangements to meet in Tiburon the next day. Jeff was thoroughly impressed with the condo, and his wife, Bonnie, and their children loved it even more than he did. They knew it was perfect for Deborah.

The following afternoon, Jeff drove his mother down to see the condo. Jennifer and Jeff's family were waiting for them outside. Deborah greeted everyone individually, and, gently laying her hand on Jennifer's forearm, she said, "I hope you haven't gone to too much trouble to find me something." Then she smiled the smile that was always a compliment to the recipient. "Well, I suppose you are all waiting for me. Let's take a look."

Leading the way up the stairs to the condo, Deborah stopped suddenly, bent down, and picked up a purple petal. "Look," she exclaimed with delight, "it's so beautiful. It's such a royal color." Delicate petals of floppy purple blossoms were strewn and crumpled on the stairs. They had fallen from the tree that grew beside the staircase. "They're everywhere," Deborah said, handing Jennifer the petal, "like so many rose petals."

"It's so soft," Jennifer said, "like some kind of fabric."

"Yes," Deborah murmured as she stepped into the entry hall, "like silk."

As her family toured the house, happily discovering an array of features, comforts, and advantages in every room, Deborah followed quietly. She smiled gently but said little as they pointed out the quality of the carpets, the placement of the skylights, the elegance of the custom-made shutters, and the recessed marble fireplace in the living room.

In the living room, Deborah, a petite figure, made her first real comment. She looked around her and then up at the high ceilings and said, "I feel so small."

"But, Mother, look at the light," Jeff answered.

"Deborah, come out on the balcony," Bonnie said. "You have to look at this view!"

Jennifer joined the others on the balcony and, with her practiced agent's eye, noted that it was protected from the wind on both sides and glassed in below the railing. The view was indeed magnificent: A gentle swell of green grass extended a few hundred feet to a narrow road bordering the shoreline. Next to the road was a walking path, and then the gentle lapping surf and expansive clarity of the Bay cradled between Angel Island and Belvedere Island, showcasing a view of the skyline on the other side of San Francisco Bay.

Standing next to the railing, wearing a sober, almost worried expression, Deborah said without enthusiasm, "Yes, it is a grand view." Then she leaned slightly forward and looked down below. There was a smile on her face when she turned back. "Look at that," she said with real pleasure. "Isn't that nice? A tree just like the one in front."

Everyone looked over the railing at the tree with purple blossoms.

"Jennifer, do you know what variety of tree that is?" she asked.

"I'm sorry, Deborah, I don't. But I'll find out."

Bonnie opened the sliding doors on the other side of the living room and invited Deborah to look at the view from that angle. With her same quiet smile, Deborah said, "Yes, dear, I can see it from here. The tree, Jennifer, you must be sure to find out the type of tree. Just for me."

After the tour, Jeff helped his mother into his car and walked back to say goodbye to Jennifer. As they shook hands in farewell, Jennifer whispered, "Does she like it?"

"I can't really tell," Jeff answered. "We'll have a chance to talk some more on the drive back, and I'll call you tonight."

That evening, between trivial tasks like filling the paper-clip dispenser and arranging her pencils and pens,

Jennifer paced her office as she waited for the call. When the phone finally did ring, she jumped.

Jeff's first sentence was a tense question. "Jennifer, remember the tree that Mother liked? Do you know the name of that tree?"

The first thing Jennifer had done upon getting home was to call Victor. "Yes, it's a pleroma, sometimes called princess flower. Native to Brazil—"

"Wonderful," he said with a sigh of relief. "Mother wants the pleroma tree, and the condo that goes with it."

$$ℙ \quad ℭ$$

The next day Victor called Jennifer to find out if his horticultural tip had made any difference.

"I'll say it did. The tree that Deborah showed me, and that you later identified, sold the house."

He chuckled and replied, "Maybe next time you'll run across a wishing well that will make things even easier."

The response on the other end of the line was not what he expected.

In a serious tone Jennifer said, "Victor, I'm serious. This is one of my very favorite sales, but I really don't feel like I can take credit for it."

"Of course you can. You're just not looking in the right place. Following a sale there should of course be time for looking around and understanding all the things that sold the product, sorting through the things that you did and the things that other people did. You should allot a modest amount of time to identifying the features that kept the customer interested and the feature that excited the customer the most, but it doesn't matter one bit whether it was you or the customer who found the feature first. Because, more than selling a product, you facilitated the meeting and the spirit of the sale. You brought together a customer and a product as surely as if you had been a matchmaker, and your good judgment, knowledge, and timely encouragement made it possible for something to take place that exceeded the expectations of everyone involved."

Jennifer had not said a word.

"Jennifer, are you still there?"

"I'm still here. But—"

"Jennifer, the fact that it is one of your favorite sales is the reason you feel you can't take credit for it. Leave the conquering-hero scenario for someone else. That's nothing but fodder for the ego. Instead, take credit for your role as a guide and your ability to discover inherent wisdom in the purchase of something new and perfectly suitable for Deborah. You see, with the best sellers a sale happens so smoothly that no one, including themselves, can accurately explain the process. But beginning or unskilled sellers are so eager to take things into their own hands that they often find themselves the center of attention. Which is unfortunate, because that's where the customer should be."

"Thank you, dear. Now I must run along and open an escrow."

Victor hung up the phone with a laugh.

He is somebody who never claimed much for himself. People just kind of gave it to him. His shadow never ate him alive.

—John Tarrant on Roshi Aitken

❧ 7 ❧

Secret Plan of a Sales Legend

Goals are the substance and reality of any plan. A plan is a step-by-step process. Successfully completing each step is a goal. You must complete smaller goals to achieve larger ones. That is finally what makes any plan work.

Sometimes you get overambitious and set goals too far ahead. Goals that illuminate the horizon without shedding light on the present are not very useful. They will mislead rather than keep you on track.

Sometimes goals are blurry because they lack specifics. You may plan to break a bad habit, start a new business, or increase sales, but without specifying the how, when, and what, all you have is a good idea, and nothing really happens.

Sometimes goals become their own fascination. You may find yourself focusing on the goal down the road, but if you don't pay proper attention to the steps you must take to get there, you may end up stumbling. Every step counts to complete any plan or journey.

All goals and plans are made and completed today. Today you may make plans for tomorrow, but today you do what you planned yesterday. No matter what the circum-

stances, you never get past today. Being mindful of this re-
inforces the realness of the goals you set, whether it's winning a game, climbing a mountain, living a productive life,
or making the next sale.

ၮ   ၡ

Every year on the first day of fall, Carrie and I have the pleasure of dining at Victor's to celebrate the change of the sea-
son. This year, Victor and his friend Jennifer prepared a
luscious cream of watercress soup and a golden soufflé followed by apple mousse with apple brandy sauce. Following
dinner, Victor wasn't the least bit modest as he carefully un-
corked a rare Trockenbeerenauslese.

As we sat around marveling at the wine and talking
about nothing in particular, Carrie casually observed that
Bryan was the only other person that she could imagine
serving such a splendid wine.

"Who's Bryan?" Jennifer asked.

Victor smiled. I had introduced the two men several
years ago, and, since that time, they had become good
friends. I set the tall, thin wineglass on the dark mahogany
tabletop and explained that Bryan was one of the two greatest salespeople I had ever known.

I first met Bryan when I was selling hi-fi and going to
grad school. He was bright and intense, and that was part of
his sales genius. Intensity, in fact, was Bryan's whole
lifestyle. For relaxation back then he climbed rocks, *big* rocks
like Half Dome in Yosemite. For transportation he bought
the only Alfa Romeo Montreal in the United States, knowing
full well he couldn't register it. For vacation reading he

chose *Finnegan's Wake* and the Sutras. He wore jodhpur boots, drank vintage wine, and was addicted to Tic-Tac breath mints. He had all the quirks and class of a living sales legend.

His sales exploits and intense charisma captured the attention of a young, burgeoning industry. In fact, it was not unusual for other companies to send their salespeople to mystery shop him, hoping to pick up some secret of his success. He sold at a time when there were no video products to speak of and very little car stereo, which meant that his sales were confined mostly to home audio components.

Without exception, he sold $80,000 to $90,000 worth of audio components every December. To date, his best Christmas had been $93,000, with respectable gross profit, but he considered that a disappointing performance. Although nobody in the consumer electronics industry had ever sold that much in a single month, Bryan had his own "century club," and no matter how he figured it, $93,000 was not $100,000.

I remember his telling me that December 1973 was going to be different. He wasn't going to bother figuring out how; he was just going to do it. With Bryan I knew there would be plenty of figuring and planning, but I knew what he meant. When a champion entered the Super Bowl or set foot on center court at Wimbledon or awaited the flag at Indianapolis, it was then a matter of just doing it.

Bryan often said that he had no reason to come to the store except to sell. He didn't come to buy—he already owned a hi-fi—and he didn't come to socialize with the rest of the staff; he had plenty of friends outside the store.

"You've got to be here in every way possible, with extraordinary presence of mind and body. Be here and there at the same time." He would point to a group of salespeople that always gathered near the front door. "You've got to be able to greet the customer on the other side of those salespeople and draw the customer directly to you." That was, at once, Bryan's plan and his idea of fun.

Perfect focus, timing, total involvement . . . something that the great basketball player Bill Walton called "being in the flow."

Bryan's plan did not allow for the usual retail procrastination. If you took too long checking stock in the stockroom, counting spiffs, or perusing yesterday's invoices, you could lose a sale. That stuff should have been done before or after hours. And there was no time in Bryan's day for sloppy or casual moves. If you turned your head at the wrong time, took too long listening to your own demo material, got caught on the register side of the counter, had a long lunch or dinner, or took time to finish an anecdote or a phone call when a customer entered the door, you risked losing business.

There was a company rumor that Bryan made sales before the store opened. Then one day, three of us returned from an early-morning sales meeting, and there was Bryan talking to a customer on the sidewalk, writing down something in the little leather notebook that he always carried in his back pocket. Bryan and his customer stepped aside while the assistant manager unlocked the door, then the customer followed Bryan into the store and bought a $2,000 system. I was just a little bit in awe; making a big sale before the store opened was a great way to start the day.

My biggest surprise about Bryan was finding out that he worked almost as hard before and after store hours as he did while he was on the floor. I came to work early one Friday morning and, climbing the worn stairs to the stockroom, heard Bryan talking to a customer. There was no mistaking that broadcast-quality voice. "John, remember, it's your decision, but I agree, it would be the perfect gift for your daughter. Your gift will always be a special memory to her."

When I reached the top of the stairs and rounded the corner, I found him pacing in front of the stock bench, which was covered with notated invoices. The telephone base dangled from the fingertips of his left hand while he cradled the receiver between his cheek and shoulder and took notes with his right hand. "Remember, Saturday is the busiest day of the week. . . . Sunday? Two o'clock in the afternoon would be perfect. . . . I'm looking forward to meeting her. Her name is Amy, right? I'll see you then." As he hung up the phone, he turned to me and said, "Good morning, Stan. In a little early today."

"Good morning." Then, feeling almost as if I were prying, I asked, "Were you doing some good old-fashioned telephone follow-up?"

"Following up . . . selling . . . call it what you will." He seemed just a little embarrassed, maybe because it was out of fashion (for all the wrong reasons) or maybe because it was too professional for the charismatic, seat-of-the-pants, superstar image that he managed to project with such aplomb.

"Tell you what," he said, turning and looking me directly in the eyes. "I won't tell people how you do business if you won't tell how I do mine. Okay?"

I agreed and asked him to tell me more. I knew I wasn't the seller he was, but I knew enough to recognize an opportunity to learn.

"You call every customer personally within forty-eight hours of the sale," he began. "Call to find out how much they are enjoying their system or component. 'Enjoy' is the key word here, and no purchase is too small for a call. Small sales create big ones, and big ones mean a lot more small ones. Whenever you do a record amount of business in any one month, you better optimize it if you're going to do great business for the rest of the year. Remember, 'How are you enjoying what you bought?' Not what I sold you, but what you bought.

"Ostensibly, you didn't call to ask for referrals or more sales, but of course you know more business is inherent in every follow-up call, and it's up to you to make appropriate suggestions based on what the customer told you during the initial sale. You should have heard, and made note of, who had a system they liked, or who had a system they didn't like, or who would like to have a system like they were buying. Those are all leads, things that you remember, things that you don't let get past you in the excitement of a single sale."

Bryan paused, stretched his shoulders up and down to relax the muscles. "I'll tell you something, Stan. This store is full of single-invoice mentalities. It's pathetic, but it's also your advantage. Most salespeople don't follow up for two reasons: first, because it means more work and they probably got a sales job in the first place because they didn't like hard work and, second, they don't have confidence in what or how they sold the customer initially, so why should they call the customer and risk confronting a problem? That's the working premise of a nonseller.

"What the average salesperson doesn't understand is: If the customer hasn't already called you, whatever problem there is can't be too urgent. Chances are very good that it's something you can solve on the phone, like adjusting a balance control or switching a wire from plus to minus. That's a problem that's exactly the right size to make you a hero. And since less than one percent of salespeople do any kind of consistent follow-up, you're a hero with a winner's advantage: doing something that works that nobody else bothers to do. Just one more thing, and it's important."

Bryan took a breath, and looked at me with an expression that said, "Should I continue?" I nodded.

"When you're done making your calls in the morning, sell something as soon as possible. I don't care what it is—a cassette, record cleaner, speaker wire, it doesn't matter. Establish momentum immediately. And when you're done making your calls at night, go to bed and get a good night's sleep. Get as much rest as you can. It's December, which means you don't celebrate until January. Eat well before and after work, with a snack sometime during the day. Drink lots of water, and swallow as much vitamin C as your body will tolerate. And if you have any time left over, go find a spot where you can daydream and listen to yourself breathing without being disturbed or read a book that will stir your soul."

He put both hands on his hips and squared his shoulders. "Got it?"

I nodded. Bryan smiled and gave me a pat on the shoulder to seal the confidence he had shared.

With his shoulder-length hair and well-cropped beard, he looked like one of the Three Musketeers, and I felt like D'Artagnan. He glanced at his nondescript, stainless-steel Rolex, took out a container of Tic-Tacs, gave us both one, and said, "The store's open, and we're in the wrong place."

I followed him down the stairs and watched as he walked up to a customer, shook hands, and ushered him into one of the sound rooms. There was no hesitation in his manner; it was almost as if he and the customer had an appointment. I was the only one in the store that now knew it *was* an appointment.

In December 1973, Bryan sold $102,000 worth of hi-fi equipment, a record that stood as long as that company stayed in business.

℘   ℘

I told Carrie, Victor, and Jennifer that I was always impressed by the one hundred and two. It was the two that made it a goal achieved, a record set, and a month I will never forget.

"What's Bryan doing now?" Jennifer asked.

"He owns a vineyard in Mendocino," I answered, "just like he always said he wanted. Every year he wins a record number of gold medals. It was part of the plan."

℘   ℘

I recall Bryan taking off his watch one day and handing it to me. He tapped the crystal and said, "Look at my watch and tell me, what is the second hand doing?"

"Is this a trick question?" I asked.

"I don't know."

"The second hand is circumscribing a minute of time, or encircling the numerals 1 through 12 sixty times and giving us the measure of an hour of time. Or maybe its goal is simply movement, a kind of mechanized decoration. It would depend on who's looking at it. For someone else it might be a timekeeper of inscrutable accuracy. What's the second hand to you?"

"Stan, to me the second hand is just that. It's a second hand. The reason that it's on that watch is because it ticks off seconds one second at a time. It doesn't measure minutes or hours; it measures seconds. Whatever I do or accomplish in this life is one second at a time. We would be better off if we celebrated more seconds, rather than days or years or millenniums. We would also have more fun being wherever we presently and inextricably are in the grand context of time."

I handed his watch back to him. As he slipped it on his wrist and closed the clasp, he looked up at the ceiling and said, "Someday I want to have more land than I know what to do with, because it would be something like having more time than I know what to do with, and I've never afforded myself that luxury. To me, land is something like time. . . . If I had more land than I knew what to do with, I would have time to do something good. Does that sound like a plan, Stan?"

The smile on his face was far more knowing than it had a right to be in those early years.

*Knock on the sky
and listen to the
sound!*

—*Zen saying*

❦ 8 ❧

Give Yourself a
Second Chance

"You never get a second chance to make a good first impression." This truism is part of almost every sales seminar, every parent's lecture to the children, and every guidance counselor's advice to young job seekers — for one very good reason: It's true.

To test the power of this familiar phrase, take a moment right now and think about the person you know and love the best. Can you remember the first time you saw him or her? It doesn't matter whether you first met yesterday or thirty years ago; you can't forget that first impression even if you try. It's always there, ready to be instantaneously recalled, a visual standard that you will use to measure other people in your life.

And yet, if we are wise, we temper this classic bit of advice with a clear-eyed look at the obverse. Sometimes we expect too much of ourselves and the people we meet. We allow bad first impressions to serve as excuses for not reassessing situations or giving people a second chance. After a bad first impression, we make an instantaneous decision: We've heard it, seen it, tasted it, felt it, and don't like it; now it's time to move on to something else. Relying fully on first impressions is shortsighted and self-defeating. It is also unfair.

Think about those times when things just didn't happen right: when you dressed for the occasion but everything came all undone before you got there, when everything you said was wrong, when you smiled but should have looked concerned, when you said yes and should have said no, or when you gave a presentation that you rehearsed one too many times and it came out sounding as cold and canned as Spam. Remember those bad first impressions; then take a moment and thank the people who were generous and wise enough to give you a second chance.

Salespeople sometimes have a tendency to be stingy with second chances. When you get off on the wrong foot, it's very easy to sit down and stop trying rather than looking for another way in. Worse, when customers don't meet your expectations or fit a preconceived notion, you may stop communicating and start condescending without even realizing it.

If you let first impressions rule your life, you are sure to misunderstand more than you understand and do more judging than accepting, which means you will experience less rather than more. That means you live less, and that's not the idea of selling . . . or of anything else!

The next time you get a *good* first impression, take it for what it's worth and see how it stands up. The next time you get a *bad* first impression, back up, do a little empathizing, and give that person or that situation another chance.

They say you make your own movie. Take time for a second take, just in case. It's the least you can do.

℘ ℘

Recently, an incident made me stop and weigh the relative importance of first impressions. Victor had called to ask if I would like to take a spin in his new car. Within a few minutes he pulled up in the driveway sitting behind the wheel of a red 1962 Mark II Austin Healey. The top was down, and he was grinning from ear to ear like a kid.

"Hop in. I'll give you a ride."

I got in the car, feeling the stretch of the leather as I rested back against the seat. The smell of the car was unique to vintage automobiles, a mixture of well-oiled machinery, high-octane fuel, and polished fittings. As he gently pressed the accelerator, accentuating the smooth, restrained rap of the engine, Victor said, "What do you think?"

"Beautiful," I said, smiling into the wind as we picked up a little speed. I asked him if Jimmy, his car broker, had found the car for him.

"No, Jimmy had nothing to do with this one. This was a Victor find. Last year my friend Jennifer invited me to an open house for a special property she had just listed."

As we approached a grade, Victor paused, shifted into overdrive, and eased the car into the fast lane.

"The house was nice, in the Maybeck tradition. Rundown, but grand enough so that you would never call it a fixer-upper. When we got to the door that apparently led to the garage, we both had to give it a good pull since it was stuck tight. It flew open, and there through a maze of cobwebs, we saw the outline of a very, very dusty Austin Healey with a torn top sitting in the middle of the dark garage. I'll never forget my first impression of that car. *This* car." He squeezed the steering wheel as if to reassure himself of its presence.

"I felt sorry for it, a beautiful vehicle stopped dead in its tracks. I felt like rushing it to an emergency ward. That was six months ago. After numerous telephone calls from here to Brazil and back, and reams of correspondence, I was finally able to register the automobile, take ownership, and begin the restoration process."

"It was worth it, Victor. The car's a beauty."

"Thanks," he said. It was getting cool, so we got out and put up the top and fastened on the side curtains, then headed back home.

We were both quiet, each in our own way savoring the pleasure of the fine machine, when suddenly out of the corner of my eye I saw a flash of movement at the edge of the freeway and then heard a loud crash near the hood of the car. Some idiot had thrown a large rock at us.

Victor pulled the car over to the side as soon as he could. He wore a pained and angry expression as if the rock had hit him. We both jumped out and started running, determined to catch the roadside vandal.

We didn't have to run too far. A young boy was cowering in some bushes down below the edge of the freeway, frightened and crying. "I'm sorry, I'm really sorry," he sobbed, "but nobody would stop and help us."

Lying on the ground beside him was a younger boy with dirty tearstains on his face. "He's my friend," the older boy said, talking as fast as he could. "We were hiking up that hill over there and he slipped and fell, and now he can't walk. I think he needs help bad, and every time I tried waving at people, they just kept driving or waved back. So I threw a rock, and I hope I didn't hurt your car too bad, mister, but he really needs help."

Looking at Victor, I knew he was trying just as hard as I to redress a righteous first impression. "Things are not always as they appear," I thought to myself. A brave kid willing to take a chance for a friend now stood in place of a vandal.

It appeared that the injured child had a sprained ankle, so we laid him lengthwise in the jumpseat. The older kid sat up front between us. As we drove the boys home, the older one said, "Mister, this is one of the nicest cars I've ever seen. I sure hope I didn't mess it up too bad."

"It's just a little dent," Victor reassured him. "You should have seen it about six months ago."

ᕓ   ᕕ

Victor waited for three months to fix that dent. One afternoon he stopped by the house on the way to the coast. I saw him pull in the driveway and went out to meet him. We both leaned back against the car, chatting and enjoying the late summer sunshine. I rubbed my thumb over the dented area and asked Victor when he was going to take care of it.

He smiled gently and told me that a little dent on an otherwise perfect Healey was a good lesson. It reminded him of a time when he thought that first impressions had some special value.

Instead, he said, you usually have to look twice to understand what you are really looking at. He named a couple of favorite paintings that hung on his walls and some books that he treasured. "They would have no value at all if they could be perceived with a passing glance or first reading. The least we can do is extend the same generosity to the people we meet.

"Too many times, on both personal and professional occasions, I've closed my mind and eyes too soon. A restaurant table became a judge's bench. A meeting was turned into a trial. Stan, I'll never forget the sound of that rock bouncing off the side of this car. It definitely made a dent all right."

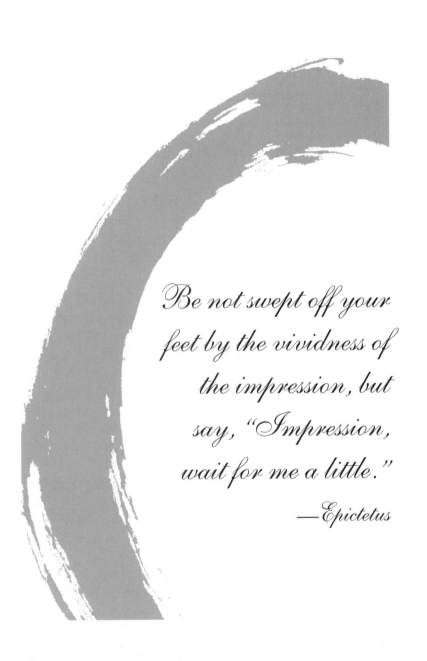

Be not swept off your feet by the vividness of the impression, but say, "Impression, wait for me a little."

—Epictetus

❦ 9 ❦

Question of Concern

I magine that after you do your very best job of presenting a special feature of your product, the customer says, "I really don't care much for that idea." No matter what the feature is or how critical it is to the product, most salespeople in that situation have the same reaction: to downplay the customer's comment or ignore it altogether.

That's a very understandable response—and a very big mistake. By saying she doesn't like "that idea," the customer is signaling you that she doesn't understand it or has a special concern about it. More than likely, that response means she's unclear how she would use it or why she needs it. By saying she doesn't like it, the customer is actually asking for clarification.

Expressing concern, even in such a roundabout way, indicates the customer has thought about your product and has an opinion. If she does *not* express her concerns, she is not doing her job as a responsible buyer.

Your job is to listen and understand those concerns, even when they sound like skeptical comments. Acknowledge your customer's puzzled expressions. Try to perceive aspects of "yes" in what you initially hear as "no," and take time to respond in a sensitive way.

It's all a matter of perspective. Imagine for a moment that you're on a plane and the captain announces, "There are a few clouds up ahead and we can expect a little turbulence, so please keep your seat belts buckled and in just a few minutes we'll turn off the sign and you'll be free to get up and walk around."

What would be your response? Would you ignore the last part of the announcement and proceed to have an anxiety attack when the plane started shaking? Probably not. Instead, you would prepare yourself for a few bumps and look forward to an otherwise smooth flight. Think of a customer's random concerns as just a few bumps on the way to making the sale.

ᕹ   ᕹ

Velma, the Vacuum Cleaner Saleslady, is an American classic. With her right hand resting protectively on the box that holds her machine, the new Neapolitan, Velma asks us to bring our current vacuum cleaner into the living room. Carrie returns with it, an old machine that will soon be nothing more than a scapegoat for a sales pitch. Its owners are not terribly concerned about its fate; a broken wheel and a tendency to go backward when you push it forward are not endearing qualities.

Velma reaches for our vacuum cleaner and asks, "What's the first thing you think of when you're buying a vacuum?"

"I don't know," I respond. "What?"

"Dirt!" she exclaims.

"Oh yes, dirt," Carrie says with a smile and not much enthusiasm.

"Yes, of course," I chime in. "Dirt."

I have memories of the dirt to which she is referring—the dirt in the water in the vacuum cleaner pan. When I was a kid, my mother owned an early model of the Neapolitan, and it was my job to take it outside and empty the dirty water. I hated it.

When I describe my childhood memory to Velma, she laughs and says, "That's silly. You just dump it down the toilet." She then proceeds to unpack her vacuum and clean several areas on the carpet.

I'm not satisfied with her solution to my problem. My mother would never have let me dump muddy water down the toilet. I'm not sure I would dump a pan full of silt down my own toilet. Why risk stopping up a toilet to save a few steps? Throw it outside where it belongs, the adult Stan thinks. But that's a miserable job, the young Stan recalls; the muddy water always splattered on my white tennis shoes when I rinsed out the pan at the faucet.

Continuing her presentation, Velma takes out her "dustfinder"—a high-intensity lamp with a short wooden handle and a metal shade—and begins to talk about air quality. She stomps on the carpet a couple of times and shines her light on the rising dust, which becomes extraordinarily visible. "It's enough to make you think twice," she says.

Making us think twice about dirt is Velma's mission. I now feel about as comfortable walking across our living room floor as across a freshly plowed field.

"Well, what do you think, Stan and Carrie?" asks Velma. We both smile and nod. "Any questions so far?" We both shake our heads.

Then Velma lifts the machine up to our eye level and trains the beam of her dustfinder on the water in the translucent tank. It's filthy. She looks at us, nodding quickly, and says, "See what I mean? Dirt!"

Carrie nods, but I don't. I ask Velma, "Who's going to empty it?"

"Stan, we'll let you do the honors since you had all that practice."

She knows how to listen, and she remembers what she heard, but she doesn't know what to do with it. She just threw my childhood memory back at me. Either it seems trivial to her, or she doesn't want to risk talking about a problem that may involve the heart of her product.

I do not move from the sofa. After a few moments of awkward silence, Velma suddenly "remembers" that she left something in her car. She'll be right back, she says.

This is intended to give us the prescribed few minutes alone to make a buying decision. Instead, that's just enough time for me to tell Carrie what I think about pulling around a bucket of muddy water and having to empty it and rinse it out every time somebody uses the vacuum. Carrie says she doesn't much like that idea, either.

Velma returns. We tell her what we've decided. When she leaves with her Neapolitan, we take the brochure, her business card, and our free gift and put them all in an inconspicuous place.

ၐ   ၡ

A couple of weeks later, when I visited Victor, his house-keeper answered the door, and I decided to get her opinion on the matter. I was asking what kind of vacuum cleaner she preferred when Victor came into the hallway.

"Stan, why the sudden interest in vacuum cleaners?" he asked in a bemused tone. So I told him all about Velma and the vacuum, and described how she had dismissed my concerns.

"You know, Stan," he said when I finished, "the door-to-door vacuum cleaner seller is such a cliché, it's tempting to completely discount what happened as some kind of joke. But in fact, that was a selling situation as legitimate as any other, and Velma blew it royally."

By this point we were seated in Victor's library. The housekeeper must have just finished in this room; the smell of lemon furniture oil filled the air.

"There are so many things Velma could have done when you complained about the water pan. She might have mentioned that the filtration system is vastly improved from the model your mother used and that the pan needs to be emptied far less often."

Trust Victor to know something like that.

"She might have showed you the new pan attachment clip system, which is easier to operate. Or—here's an idea—she might have acknowledged that you're absolutely right about its being a nuisance, but the trade-off is a much more thorough job of cleaning."

As Victor ticks off these suggestions on his fingers, I find myself nodding.

"But instead she just brushed you aside. Ignoring a customer's concerns is equivalent to hearing a person say he can't swim, then pushing him into the water and acting surprised when he shouts for help." He shook his head with dismay. "Of course, customers don't cry for help. They just use one of many variations of 'We'll think it over' and, with a perfectly insincere smile, say goodbye."

When you talk,
you repeat what you
already know; when
you listen, you often
learn something.

—Gared Sparks

10

Once Upon a Time

Salespeople sometimes complain about a bad day or a bad month as though they were on a fishing excursion. They say things like, "I don't know, it's just really been a bad month." They shake their heads as if totally confounded by the mysterious dearth of sales. It never seems to occur to them to ask themselves why some salespeople are having a good month at the same time they're having a bad month.

It's like asking a fisherman if he's having any luck. He shakes his head, mesmerized by the glimmering water, and says, "No, nothing happening today." Hang around long enough, and he might say something like, "See that guy down there? He just caught himself a big one a few minutes ago." Maybe the reason was different bait, location, equipment, or technique, or maybe he knew the fish could see the fisherman better than the fisherman could see the fish.

Both the seller and the fisherman can have good days and bad days, but I never recall being on a lake or a sales floor where there wasn't someone somewhere catching something or selling something. And you can be sure that that "someone" was doing something that everyone else wasn't.

Some fishermen wait to see if they're biting, and others go out to catch fish. Some salespeople wait for a sale to come along, and other salespeople create sales. The difference is not how much time they put in; it's how much energy they put into the time they spend. It's your choice.

ဖ   ၅

Before Bryan achieved superstar status in the consumer electronics industry, he sold hi-fi equipment at a store in the California suburb of Hayward. It was there that he met Mr. Brown, the customer who showed him the difference between taking an order and making a sale.

It was one of those slow spring days in the middle of the week that tested the patience of a sales apprentice. There were no customers in the store, and it seemed like there was nothing to do except wait for the customers to show up.

Bryan walked from one end of the store to the other, pushing buttons, adjusting balance controls, turning receivers on, turning them off. When he heard a favorite song on FM, he would go to the biggest wall system, dial it in, and turn it up till the speaker started making the crackling noises that hi-fi buffs call clipping. Finally, out of sheer boredom, he began changing the bottom speakers on one of the systems. He was connecting the wires when he heard someone quietly exclaim: "Well, would you look at *this*?"

Looking up, Bryan saw an older man with hands on his hips surveying the store. The man had a toothpick in one corner of his mouth and seemed like he was just a second away from laughing.

Bryan said, "How are you doing today?"

The man kept gazing around the store. "Lordy, I've never seen so many speakers in all my life."

"Are you looking for speakers?"

The man didn't answer. Instead, he stared at Bryan's beard. In Hayward, at that time, a beard was something that you grew as a joke during Pioneer Days. Bryan knew about "addressing objections," so, using his most diplomatic tone, he asked a straightforward question: "Does the beard bother you?"

"Son, it doesn't bother me if it doesn't bother you," the man replied. "Never had one myself. I always wondered if it would itch."

"It's never been a problem," Bryan replied. He wasn't really sure where this conversation was headed, and he didn't know what to do except keep talking. "I've known several people who started beards and shaved them off because of that very reason, but I've never had that problem."

"Is that so?" the man replied, rubbing his chin. "Well, it looks real good on you."

"Thank you." Bryan hesitated briefly, then asked, "Are you looking for a hi-fi system?"

The man laughed good-naturedly and said, "No, not me; I'm just killing time. My wife is next door checking out material for drapes. I've never been in here before, so I thought I'd come in and take a look." The man shook his head in amazement. "More speakers than I've ever seen in my life!"

"Do you have a hi-fi system now?" Bryan asked.

"No, not really. We got this old record player that doesn't work too good. Don't seem to have much time for listening to music anyway. It's a shame, really. I used to like music a lot."

"Would you like to listen to something now?"

"If you have the time. My name is Brown, by the way."

"My name is Bryan. Pleased to meet you."

"Nice to meet you, Bryan. How long you been in this line of work?"

"Not all that long," he answered. Bryan went on to tell Mr. Brown a little bit about himself and, as he talked, ushered Brown into the one of the private, soundproof demo rooms. Closing the glass doors, he invited Mr. Brown to have a seat in one of the plush swivel chairs while he picked out some music.

All the salespeople kept their own selection of records in stacks near a central desk. Bryan flipped through his pile quickly, feeling a little foolish that he hadn't asked Mr. Brown what kind of music he liked. He paused briefly at some modern jazz but quickly realized that was his own taste and probably not Mr. Brown's. When he came to an album of Montavani's greatest hits, he instinctively felt he had found it.

Returning to the demo room, Bryan discovered Mr. Brown playfully spinning around in his chair. Bryan put on the record, took the other chair, and sat back. As the music filled the room, the two men chatted quietly about this and that. When they got around to talking about hi-fi, which took awhile, Mr. Brown told Bryan, with some pride, that he had bought one of the first consoles years ago.

"Had a terrific tone, it did. When I set it right, you could hear that bass all the way down the street. Never sounded like this, though. I never heard anything like this."

For a while neither man said anything, just sat quietly and listened to the music. Bryan noticed that Mr. Brown's eyes seemed to be focused off in the distance. Suddenly, when a new selection came on, he sat up straight in the chair and turned to Bryan. His eyes sparkling, he said, "Stay right here. I'll be right back. Don't leave."

In a few minutes Mr. Brown returned, eagerly escorting a rosy-cheeked Mrs. Brown. He hustled her into the demo room and introduced her to Bryan.

"Now, Bryan, show her everything you showed me. Show her the Loudness Contour feature. Show her the two-way speakers, and how they compare to the three-way speakers. And play that same song again." As Bryan put the stylus on the cut and the sound of violins surged through the room again, Mr. Brown slipped his hand into his wife's and said, "Remember this one, honey? Doesn't it sound wonderful?"

The Browns sat in the demo room enjoying the music for more than an hour. Bryan stayed in the background, answering questions and pointing out features now and then but mostly just sharing the time, friend to friend.

An hour later, Bryan rolled out a pair of three-way speakers with a turntable, deluxe phono cartridge, cassette deck, headphone, and receiver. With a little help from Bryan, Mr. Brown had sold his wife the hi-fi. In the meantime, Mrs. Brown had found the right material for the drapes. They both looked happy with each other's accomplishments.

Both of the Browns thanked Bryan several times for being so considerate. "I know you went out of your way for us, and I really appreciate it," Mr. Brown added.

Later on, when Bryan told me that story, he said that one mild comment hit him like lightning. When Mr. Brown said "going out of your way," Bryan suddenly understood that up until then he had just been taking orders and filling out invoices.

Bryan helped the Browns load the system into their car and asked them to come back and visit him again.

Mr. Brown opened the car door for Mrs. Brown. Before she got in, he winked at her and said, "The kid's got a great beard, doesn't he?"

Bryan laughed and walked back to the store knowing he had just *created* his first sale.

ၣ   ၅

As Bryan developed his skills and discovered his special talent, he never let stereotypes or preferences of age, sex, or status limit his effectiveness. He prejudged no one. He was motivated by the presence of a customer, pure and simple. If a person was in the store and did not *sell* hi-fi, then that person was a customer and would soon be *buying* a hi-fi. It was a working assumption that allowed for no phony excuses.

On that long-ago Wednesday morning, when the store was dead quiet, Bryan could easily have assumed that Mr. Brown was just a browser and paid him only cursory attention. When Mr. Brown showed some interest in the speakers, Bryan could easily have limited his demonstration to the speakers on the main wall, since no one else was using them, rather than taking the extra step of setting up the private room. When choosing the music, Bryan could easily have selected his own favorite, rather than being sensitive to the customer's style. And, most of all, he could have directed all his remarks to the product, rather than taking the time to get to know Mr. Brown as a person and letting a genuine conversation unfold.

With his sale to Mr. and Mrs. Brown, Bryan instinctively put into action a philosophy that he only later put into
words. It became one of his main themes: *Things happen because of other things that you make happen.*

A few years later, when Bryan and I worked together, I remember going to lunch with him one day. We had asked another salesperson to join us, but he said no, he was with a
customer.

During lunch, Bryan seemed to be thinking about
something, working something out in his mind. Finally, he
put down his sandwich and said, "You know, Stan, I just
don't get it. People are always saying 'I'm with a customer'
or 'He's with a customer.' But what does that really mean?
Do they really understand what they're saying?"

He quickly took a bite of his sandwich, then answered
his own question. "I don't think they do. The point is not
where the salesman is but where the *customer* is. The customer is not wandering around the store, not even in a demo
room. The customer is not just looking or just shopping or
just thinking it over or just comparing prices. The customer
is standing in front of you, *with* you, only you, nobody else!"

Bryan took a big swallow of iced tea, to wash down the
sandwich, and rushed on. "And what is that person doing?
Buying. The customer is always *buying* from you. Is there really any other reason to think otherwise? Think about that,
Stan. If the customer is not *buying* from you, what is that
customer doing *with* you?"

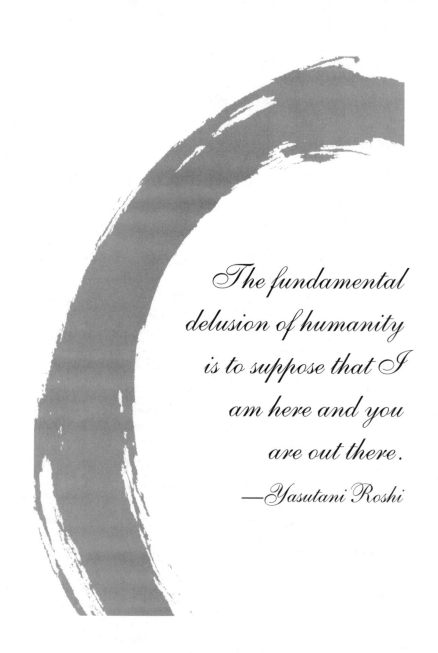

*The fundamental
delusion of humanity
is to suppose that I
am here and you
are out there.*

—*Yasutani Roshi*

11

It Takes Courage
to Sell Candy

O nce, many years ago, while waiting for a train in New York, I found myself standing near an elderly man who was leaning on a cane and smoking a meerschaum pipe with an amber stem. I commented on the classic design, and we began a conversation. Eventually he asked what I did. When I told him, he nodded, peered through some wisps of blue smoke, and said, "Next week I'll be a hundred years old, and one thing I can tell you: Don't expect life's very best unless you're giving it your very best." With that, he boarded one train, and I boarded another. We never saw each other again, but I'll never forget his words of advice.

Often the way to give life your very best is to do something different, something unique. We have become very accustomed to looking for the same answers in the same places. It takes daring and courage to try something completely new. When it works, when your courage is blended with skill, you look your best; when it doesn't, you may fall on your face and look your worst. That's the chance you take.

When a powerful new idea comes to mind, it has a taste and feeling all its own. Once you experience it, you are not really satisfied with anything less. Even if acting on your idea means breaking the rules.

It might mean giving your business card to someone who is eating dinner and doesn't want to be disturbed, or interrupting a private conversation when you're traveling and telling the people across the aisle that you just happen to sell what they're discussing.

People don't like to be surprised . . . people have a right to their privacy . . . there is a time and place for everything. All of these things may be generally true, but keeping your distance has little to do with selling.

A seller who knows how to mix courage and skill can create a feeling of intimacy at a moment's notice . . . can excite people without their permission . . . can discover opportunities at inopportune times . . . can make a person feel good about *doing* something rather than *thinking* about doing something.

Courage in a sale is sometimes just an imaginative move that didn't ask permission to happen.

ɕ   ɕ

It was a perfect day for lunch at La Petite, the little soup-and-sandwich cafe located in the Town and Country shopping center. The dozen or so customers at the sidewalk tables were as busy talking as they were eating. I couldn't help listening to fragments of nearby conversations as I finished an avocado and tomato sandwich.

A woman at the next table was explaining to her three friends that she wasn't ready for counseling or the group activities that went with it. A young man at the opposite table, wearing walking shorts and hiking boots, told his friend about a day hike that starts at seven thousand feet and ends above timberline and passes four "totally pristine" lakes along the way. His friend said she was spending next summer at Yosemite. Across the way, two little kids in soccer uniforms were spraying themselves and their parents with water guns. "Johnny? Jessamyn? Please put those away for a while," admonished the dad, pointing his finger and shaking his head. "Please don't get the other people wet."

I tossed a piece of bread to a sparrow that looked at me expectantly from the edge of the sidewalk. It caught the crumb before it landed and flew up to the red tile roof with the tiny windfall clamped in its beak.

A cool breeze blew the napkins off a couple of tables while people squinted and gazed up at the dazzling sunlight. It was a day when you were grateful for far more than the food on the table and at a loss as to how to express it.

Suddenly, a high-pitched shout shattered the mood.

"All right, ladies and gentlemen!"

I turned around in my chair, looking for the person who was so blatantly interrupting the peaceful afternoon. A kid in his early teens with thick blonde hair pulled back in a ponytail stood in the middle of the sidewalk just a few feet from my table. He wore Levis and a white T-shirt that was several fashionable inches too long, and he stood beside a large plastic container with a folding lid, which he opened as if it were a box of props. With arms spread wide, as if about to break into song, he smiled too brightly and launched into his pitch.

"How are all of you today?" he asked. "My name is Charles, and this is my part-time job. Today we are featuring peanut brittle." He laid a box of peanut brittle candy on the sidewalk.

Most of the cafe customers suddenly became intensely interested in their salads and sandwiches.

"We also have chocolate clusters. . . ." He put a box of chocolate clusters next to the peanut brittle. "And coconut fudge, and vanilla taffy, and strawberry taffy." As he spoke, he set out one box of each, carefully arranging them in one precise line. "Now you can have any one of these boxes of delicious candy for six dollars, or three boxes for only fifteen dollars!"

Nobody said or did anything. The incidental conversations came to a halt. Some customers looked like they were biting their tongues or trying not to laugh; others tried to pretend the kid wasn't there.

Charles hitched up his pants and made a real effort to maintain his broad, assertive smile as he said, "Now don't everybody all jump up at once."

Nobody made a move or said a word.

The kid began carefully putting each box back into his container. He looked up and said, with one last wide-eyed smile, "I notice some of those sandwiches you're eating have onions on them. A nice peppermint cream wafer would probably really hit the spot, and I just happen have some peppermint wafers."

A couple of people smiled when he said that, but still they didn't make eye contact. Finally, after a short embarrassed silence, the kid shrugged his shoulders and said to no one in particular: "Maybe somebody would like to try just one box." He glanced around; no one responded.

As he closed up the box, I heard him say to himself, "I tried."

Without thinking, I said, "Courage."

He looked up. "What?"

"That took courage," I explained.

"Yeah?" he asked in a tone that seemed to add "So what?"

"That was a courage sale. It'll work someday," I said, thinking more in terms of years than days.

"Thanks," he said glumly.

I started to explain that no one in my family ate candy, since my daughters were now away, then I remembered something I had been taught long ago: To satisfy a customer, you must sell them something. I was the customer, and I was watching a novitiate salesperson with a tough sale turn and walk away. "Wait a second," I said. "I'll—"

Before I could finish my sentence, he turned around and walked into the little cafe.

I watched as he walked up to the counter, put his container down, and spoke to the cashier. He took a box of peppermint wafers from his container, carefully opened it, and placed it on the counter by the cash register. I saw no money change hands. He shook the cashier's hand and walked outside with a smile that said he was in control and had a brand-new idea.

"Ladies and gentlemen," he said in a quieter voice, "I hope I didn't disturb your lunch too much. When you're finished eating, you might want to walk inside and help yourself to a free mint, courtesy of Charles."

Within seconds, four customers got up from their lunch and lined up to buy candy from Charles. I was the fourth customer. As I paid him, I said, "That was good selling."

Lowering his voice and tilting his head to one side, he said, "Thanks. It took courage."

I nodded and smiled, and when I turned around to leave, he said, "Sir?"

I turned back around, and he extended his hand. As we shook hands, he said, "It worked *today*."

ဈ   ဉ

The next day, Victor dropped by to give Carrie an out-of-print cookbook that contained a recipe that she had asked him about for years. I had put the peanut brittle in a candy dish on the coffee table, and I encouraged him to try a piece. He chewed it thoughtfully, and I told him where I had bought it.

"You paid a good price for a good story," he said. "As for the candy . . . well, the kid knew what it took to sell it. He figured if he was giving it away, everybody would take a box. He just had to figure out how to *almost* give it away. I'm sure he assumed that once they sampled one of his mints for free, they would want to buy some."

Victor reached for another tiny piece of brittle. "It's getting better," he said.

"And that was pretty good thinking," he continued, "but what he didn't count on was the generous spirit of most people. People want to be kind and help others; they just have a terrible time finding a comfortable way of doing it. So after the kid had made a last-ditch plea, asking any or all to buy just one box, he realized that he could walk away embarrassed or he could try something new, something that wasn't in any book. Even if his idea didn't work, at least he could say he truly had tried."

"And you know, Victor, for such a young person, it really was a pretty good idea."

"It was. But the real idea wasn't putting out the box of free samples. The idea was something that you gave him at exactly the right time, something called courage. It was a good idea . . . always has been."

*If you follow all
the rules, you miss
all the fun.*

—Katharine Hepburn

12

The Matchbook Matrix

Don't waste time celebrating your first sale with a customer. The *second* sale with the same customer is the one that counts. That's when the customer is saying there is something unique, appealing, or special about *you*. *You* have made something happen during the sales process that pleases her enough to want to do business with you again.

You may have spun her head and captured her heart with flawless communication skills and a winning presentation, or simply started a conversation that you both wanted to continue. Maybe you sensed a feeling and fulfilled a need with perfect timing. Whatever you did was a matter of extraordinary customer awareness, and it was good enough to begin a business relationship that will provide you with regular moral as well as financial support.

Repeat business is your only real reassurance and, in the last analysis, the only true measure of your talent and success.

ℙ ℚ

One night several years ago, I stopped off at Victor's to

return a book he had loaned me. He invited me into the library for a glass of wine.

You and I have dens; Victor has a library. The walls are an intriguing shade of green that I have never found a word for, and the chairs are soft, henna-colored leather. There must be close to a thousand books in the room, and I am quite certain Victor has read every one of them.

"I was about to start a fire," Victor said. "Hand me that book of matches, will you, Stan?"

On the shelf where he was pointing was a small faience bowl that contained a matchbook, carefully centered. It was quite old, and all the matches were gone. Why had he saved it?

"Victor, what is this?"

"Oh, not that one. That one's special. Didn't I ever tell you that story?"

On the inside cover of the match book was a hand-drawn grid with three columns and four rows containing plus and minus signs and checkmarks.

BEGIN	END	
+	+	✓ ✓ ✓ ✓
−	−	
−	+	✓ ✓
+	−	

"Okay," I said, "I give up. What is it?"

"I've always thought of it as the matchbook matrix." As he found some more matches and got a roaring fire going, Victor proceeded to tell me the story.

In 1959, Victor had a lengthy meeting with a big investor in the hills above Berkeley, California. Victor was quite young then, much younger than his client, but the meeting was successful, and it meant a substantial commission. To celebrate, Victor decided to head down to Telegraph Avenue and browse around. He happened into a combination framing shop and gallery and began idly shuffling through the bins of prints.

He almost missed it. Tucked in between several large prints was a beautiful piece that Victor immediately realized was no ordinary print. It turned out to be a Miro estampe marked with the ridiculously low price of $12.

Victor offered to pay more, since clearly it had been mispriced, but the proprietor refused. "No, it was your good eye and your good luck. I'm happy for you. By the way, I'm Jason, the owner."

Jason was genuinely delighted at Victor's good fortune. He offered Victor a cup of espresso (in those days, a rare and somewhat exotic treat) and a Gauloise cigarette. It seemed a perfect complement to finding the print: a French cigarette, a fine cup of coffee, and a few minutes of friendly conversation between two art lovers.

Jason lit the two cigarettes and then quickly wrote something on the inside cover of the matchbook. Victor couldn't resist asking about it.

"It's part of my own unique system of improving business," Jason said. "I don't have much money for advertising, so I have just one way to help the business grow."

"And that is . . . ?" Victor asked.

"People. I figure the only way I can build the business is to treat people right. And the only way I can tell if I'm doing that is to keep score. So this is what I do."

He showed Victor the matchbook—the same one I now held in my hands—and explained his scoring system of pluses and minuses.

Jason had figured out that the real business of selling was a simple matter of completing a memorable, worthwhile conversation. And he had determined that there were just four kinds of conversations: those that began well and ended well (plus/plus), those that began and ended badly (minus/minus), those that started out well and ended badly (plus/minus), and those that began badly and ended up well (minus/plus).

"That last one's the hardest kind," Jason said. "It takes hard work to turn a frown into an expression worth remembering. Of course, sometimes people bring a rotten mood with them and there's nothing I can do to change it. I feel bad about that. But the worst dilemma is when things start off well and then turn sour. Fortunately, that doesn't happen too often."

"So each of these check marks represents a sale?" Victor asked.

"Oh, no. They represent good conversations. If the whole encounter is positive, I know I'll sell something to that person again—if not today, then sometime later. You, for instance—do you think you'll buy something else from me again?"

"Of course," Victor said.

"Then you get a check mark in the plus/plus column. And since it's almost closing time, you also get these. Tomorrow's a brand-new day." He gave Victor the matchbook. "Enjoy your Miro."

Over the next twenty or so years, Victor did thousands of dollars' worth of business with Jason. Victor became a serious collector, and his knowledge of art expanded greatly. But none of his pieces, he said, ever seemed quite as magical as the little Miro.

Since Victor told me that story, I think about that matchbook every time I encounter a consumer survey, customer audit form, questionnaire, or some other standard form of market research. In spite of their claims of statistical validation and their high cost, none of them ever compares to the matchbook matrix. Jason had distilled many complex methods into a marvel of simplicity, but, even more important, he had started a relationship that would be remembered far longer than any product.

ℙ ℭ

About a year later Victor and I were sitting on his balcony, which takes in a panoramic view of the Golden Gate Bridge. The sun was low in the sky, and a bright reflection spread out toward the ocean horizon. Victor squinted behind a pair of old aviator sunglasses as he paced back and forth with his favorite Peterson pipe in one hand and a letter from Jason in his other hand. Jason was ill, and this, as it turned out, would be one of his last correspondences.

Victor had been doing some serious reflecting that afternoon. "I went from biomorphic abstraction to abstract expressionism with Jason," he said. "Wherever I traveled, I brought back something for Jason, and he would do the same for me. Estampes from Paris and prints from New York, really nothing more than souvenirs there, but I shared a couple of treasures with him that I found in the counting house of Plandiura in Catalonia. Those brought tears to his eyes.

"You know, Stan, the marvelous things that you buy and collect are supposed to enrich your life, and of course they do, but finally it is the person who finds them for you or sells them to you that makes your investment truly priceless. Whether you're the seller or the buyer, that's worth remembering."

He went down to the wine cellar and returned with a Le Pin that had long been just a rumor at retail. He pulled the cork without asking if I would stick around to share it with him. That's the kind of afternoon it was, independent and solitary, when you watch the sun go down and think of things that almost last a lifetime.

*A businessman
is a hybrid of a
dancer and a
calculator.*
—Paul Valery

❦13❧

The Viewpoint
of the Customer

When was the last time your customers thanked you for helping them find the right thing? When that happened, do you suppose you sold something or did your customers buy it? The answer is obvious: They bought it. You just showed them the way.

It's a matter of how you look at it. In your mind, is the "customer" a person with feelings or a decision maker with dollars? Is the customer your opponent or your partner? What is your main objective—to close the customer or to provide the customer with the right product?

When you're with the customer, do you try to get to know the person, or are you showing how much you know about your product? Are you genuinely communicating, or are you wondering when the customer will stop talking so you can start selling? Do you plan what you're going to do *to* the customer or *with* the customer?

In a good sale, nobody does anything *to* anyone. You're doing something so well that people thank you and ask you to do it again.

℘   ℘

Carrie and I had been promising ourselves a new front door
for about fifteen years, but for one reason or another we
never seemed to get to it. We might have waited another fifteen years had it not been for Brad.

Carrie met Brad when she was almost ready to give up.
She had decided this was the year to finally do something
about the door, but her preliminary research did not go well.
Whenever she inquired about doors, the salesperson either
asked who her contractor was or handed her a brochure.
She was repeatedly brushed off, talked down to, patronized,
and generally discouraged. *Keep her in the dark and maybe
she'll disappear* seemed to be the general approach.

Then one day, while she was shuffling through some
hinged samples, a friendly young man approached and said
with a smile, "You look confused. Could you use some help?"
Carrie came out of her shopper's stupor and said yes, she
could. As they talked, Carrie quickly saw that choosing a
door was more complex than she had realized. Brad offered
to drop by the house the following day to talk with both of us.

I was skeptical at first—what's the big deal about a
door? I thought—but two minutes with Brad showed me
how wrong I was.

"The front door is the first thing visitors see when they
come to your house," he said. "It tells a lot about how people feel about their home."

All the while he talked, Brad was running his hands
carefully over our door, like a doctor examining a patient,
quietly and respectfully.

"It's amazing. Some people will spend thousands of dollars remodeling their entryway and then have their neighbor put on the door. I guess that's all right. I mean, it's their business. Some people don't care about quality. But if you *do* care, you need to have the right door."

Brad's enthusiasm was as genuine and bright as his red hair and easy smile. We assured him we did care, and he proceeded to teach us about doors.

We learned the difference between custom-made and manufactured doors. We saw and felt the textures of many different woods. We heard an interesting discourse on the history of various door designs and which ones are appropriate for which types of architecture. We learned all about floating panels and trim styles. We got a thorough lesson in different types of locks and the many possibilities of hardware, in terms of both style and finish.

Before Brad, I would have bet that no one could get excited about the different types of doorknobs. Appreciating beautiful wood is easy; it takes a true craftsman to care so intensely about the small details like locks and hardware.

Brad was thoroughly prepared with photos and samples. "Now here's a kind of doorknob you might like," he said. "It's shaped sort of like an egg, rather than completely round."

I took the sample he held out. It had a nice solid heft and fitted beautifully into my palm. "I love the way this feels in my hand. But I don't know. . . . I'm used to the lever we've always had."

"That's another way to go," Brad said. "Here's a few to look at."

And that's the way things went all morning. Brad presented all the options, outlining the pros and cons of each, but insisted we make the final decisions. "This is your door, not mine; you're going to be living with it the rest of your life."

Carrie and I agonized over the finish for the hardware. Bronze, with its slightly aged look, seemed more appropriate for the outside; on the other hand, gleaming brass seemed right for the inside. We practically begged Brad to tell us which to choose. With a pleasant smile, he said, "No, you decide."

In the end, we opted for a custom-made door of Honduran mahogany. From Brad we had learned that mahogany is resilient in damp climates, and we also felt it went well with the existing redwood trim in our entryway. We settled on a Baldwin mortised lock with a quick-release safety latch for emergency exits. And we decided to have two styles of hardware: brass for the inside, bronze for the outside.

Several days later, Brad returned to install our door. When the door was hung and the hardware and lock installed, it turned out that Carrie and I had one last decision to make. "Okay now," Brad asked, "do we want a bronze or brass peephole?"

He was holding a shiny brass tube upright in his hand. I was thinking that I actually wanted it to be bronze on the outside and brass on the inside, but before I had a chance to say it, Brad reached in his pocket, took out a bronze peephole, combined the two, and gave me more than I thought I could have.

Carrie and I spent that evening exchanging seats on the sofa to get the best view of our new door. It was picture perfect.

ℙ ℚ

The next time Victor paid us a visit, he still had his hand on the door when I opened it. "It's a pleasure to touch," he said. "He did a beautiful job, didn't he?"

Victor swung the heavy door gently back and forth and ran his fingers down the edge and around the trim as I told him all about Brad.

"You know, as he was leaving he dropped his drawknife and said something that I'll never forget. 'Some days you drop your tools,' he said, almost blushing. 'Other days you catch the pencil when it falls from your ear. . . . That's when you know you're ready.'

"I don't think Brad knew he was a consultant building a partnership with a client," I told Victor. "And I'm sure he never heard of a 'five-step selling cycle' or 'quantifying solutions.' But what he was doing, intuitively, was selling at its best."

After we were seated in the living room, Victor noticed that Carrie and I both glanced often in the direction of our new door. "You know," he said, "Brad did four things essential to the mastery of selling.

"First, he helped you"—nodding to Carrie—"when others ignored you, letting his intuition guide him. Two, he knew there was really nothing to sell until he found out, truly, what you wanted. Three, he was able to share his enjoyment of his craft with you. In fact, he probably couldn't have kept himself from doing it if he wanted to. People who love what they're doing instill that love in others. And, four, he knew what he was talking about. What you saw and heard was years of research and practice reduced to a few hours."

"And most of all," I said, "I think it was that he involved us in every step of the process. He didn't just sell us a door. He showed us how to *buy* a door."

"Exactly," Victor answered. "It was a classic case of 'with,' not 'to.'"

When Victor left that evening, Carrie and I walked him to the front door. He grasped the egg-shaped knob and said appreciatively, "Now that's wonderful. I love the way that feels in my hand."

As we were closing the door, we heard Victor comment quietly to himself, "Of course—brass inside, bronze outside." When we looked through the peephole, we saw him wink in farewell.

*If one is master
of one thing and
understands one thing
well, one has at the
same time, insight into
and understanding of
many things.*

— *Vincent van Gogh*

ℱ14℈

The Way It Should Be

When you first say hello to a customer, you are doing far more than acknowledging that person's presence. You are welcoming the customer into your life.

Introducing yourself and learning the customer's name is the purest and best way to make the customer feel comfortable.

With a simple exchange of names, you build a bridge that you and your customers cross to find common ground. You are giving them reason to believe that you are someone worth meeting, someone they will feel comfortable knowing. At the same time, you are asking them to share their private feelings about things they like and don't like.

When customers feel right about you, they will entrust you with the details of their dreams. Then you have the opportunity to put things in place for a long-lasting working relationship.

The simple truth of the matter is: You have enough time, starting with hello, to start something so satisfactory that it will never end. That's your talent, and that's your business.

ℰ ℭ

In the estimation of some of the world's most notable musicians and also of some pretty laudable critics, Village Music in Mill Valley, California, is the world's best record store. In addition to those round things that spin around and make a lot of people's lives complete, there is a collector's assortment of videos, songbooks, comics, posters, and current and back issues of music periodicals. These are some of the things you can buy, but it's actually what's *not* for sale that keeps you feeling special about being where you are.

The clientele is a pretty eclectic group, with people like B. B. King, Carl Perkins, Carlos Santana, Naomi Judd, Elvis Costello, Nick Lowe, Mel Torme, John Lee Hooker, and Ry Cooder as regulars, not including drop-in luminaries like Mick Jagger.

Today, as I walk in the store, the owner, John Goddard, waves. He has an album in one hand and reaches for the receiver of a Mickey Mouse telephone with the other while stepping over a couple of cardboard boxes stuffed with records. As always, he's wearing a T-shirt. This one is emblazoned with the store logo—a smiling visage of Cab Calloway and his immortal greeting, "Hi De Ho."

"Hey Stan," John says when he gets off the phone, "where ya been?"

"Traveling."

"Anyplace exciting?"

"L.A."

"Lucky you," he says with a chauvinistic grin. "Buy the new Jimmy Scott album."

"Good?"

"It's great."

Gary, at the register, says, "Hi, Stan. Had a chance to listen to the new Danny Gatton album yet?"

"Not really. Probably tonight."

Over in the nostalgia section, Eugene is stocking al-
bums. He smiles and says, "Pretty great party the other
night, huh?"

I smile and nod. "It was wonderful." He's referring to
the twenty-third anniversary party John gave for musician
friends and a legion of loyal customers who are unofficially
called "friends of the store." It was held at the local night-
club, Sweetwater, and it was a very special evening. Only
once in a lifetime will you have the pleasure of hearing John
Lee Hooker, Albert Collins, Robert Ward, Carlos Santana,
and Ry Cooder playing on the same stage at the same time.

I meander off to the other side of the store. The interior
of Village Music is one giant wall-to-wall, floor-to-
ceiling collage of treasured musical memorabilia that makes
most "merchandising concepts" seem sanitized and affected. Every wall and every square inch of the ceiling are
layered and hung with rare inscribed records, picture discs,
gold records, autographed black and white photographs,
vintage magazine covers, and life-size cutouts of famous
show business and music personalities.

You can be a customer for twenty-five years, like me,
and still find yourself looking at a brand-new piece of memorabilia. No sooner do I think this than I look up from one of
the bins and find myself peering at a mug shot of Janis
Joplin taken by the Berkeley police, juxtaposed with photos

of her in a sequined dress alongside a handwritten note.

Around the corner there's a poster advertising James Brown at the Apollo next to a Hank Williams poster with the reminder, "If the good Lord's willing and the creek don't rise, I'll see you at Canton Memorial Auditorium on New Year's Day 1953." And to my left, past three or four thousand records, there is a Philco Predicta, the TV with the revolving stand-alone screen that didn't exactly set a trend. The silent green screen, an immaculate relic of the 1950s, watches me as I browse for . . . hmm, I think with a smile, it's not unusual to forget what I came in here for.

It occurs to me that this is the first time I've smiled since I started shopping today. It's early afternoon, and I've already been shrugged off by an audio/video salesperson who told me I was in the wrong department, yelled at by an officious postal clerk, and left on terminal hold by someone at a tire store who had told me to be sure and ask for him.

I walk back to the register, where John, Gary, and Eugene are still talking about the big party.

"McCracklin sure stretched out his set," Gary says. "I mean he was *great* but—"

"Do you know why McCracklin played for an hour and a half?" John asks.

We all shake our heads.

"He was waiting for Ry, who was an hour late. So he keeps playing and waiting for this white boy that wants to play with him. In the meantime, John Lee, who's next, is ready to go home, and I'm trying to convince him he'll go on in a just a couple of minutes and Ry is not even there yet."

Although John shakes his head with exasperation, he

clearly enjoys talking about the producer part of his life. Suddenly he looks past the three of us toward the front door. It's a Dutch door, and the top half is always open. A woman has just pushed open the bottom half and is approaching the counter, looking a bit lost. She holds a leather handbag in one hand and the hand of a little girl in the other.

John's eyes light up. "Hello," he says, with a smile that immediately gives the customer permission to relax. "What can I do for you?"

Gary and Eugene find something to do, and I walk over to the periodical rack.

"I'm wondering if you have a copy of the *Mary Poppins* record from the movie. I have a copy, but it's so scratched up that I really can't use it."

John shakes his head and says, "I wish I could help you, but I haven't seen a clean copy of the movie version of *Mary Poppins* in a while. Is it for something special?"

"My daughter is in a dance class," she says, looking down at the little girl, whose eyes are level with the counter and floating from one curious detail to another. "At the end of the year all of the dance classes in the studio put on a big performance at the Civic Center, and we need the record so we can tape it since the dance studio uses a tape recorder for the performance. They said if anyone would have it, you would."

"Sounds pretty exciting," John says, looking at the daughter, who wipes her bangs from her eyes and unconsciously does a quick shuffle-ball-and-change. "Hey, that's pretty good," he says. He pauses while he tries to think of an option. "I wish I could help you. The only thing I can think of is you might want to try—wait a second. Stan!"

I've been staring at the magazine and listening in on the conversation, but I'm startled to hear my name come up. "Yes?"

"You have a couple of daughters."

"Yeah."

"Do they listen to *Mary Poppins*?"

Why didn't I think of this? "They used to. You're looking for a clean copy of *Mary Poppins*?" I ask the woman, trying to pretend I haven't been eavesdropping.

"To record," she answers, her eyes open expectantly. The daughter also has her eyes trained on me.

I take down the woman's name and phone number. As I make arrangements to meet her at the studio with my mint copy of *Mary Poppins*, John says with a grin, "I knew Stan could help you out."

The woman thanks me, and she and her daughter walk out smiling. John laughs to himself, clearly enjoying the contrivance. Then, looking behind me, he says, "I think someone's trying to get your attention."

I turn around and catch a glimpse of the little girl looking over the edge of the Dutch door. "Stan?"

"Yes?"

"Thanks," she giggles, then turns with a jump and runs off to catch up with her mom.

"See, Stan, it feels good to do something for someone once in a while."

"You're a heck of a producer," I reply.

"Thank you, Stan," he says, putting a serious spin on my sarcasm. He puts a copy of the Jimmy Scott album on the counter without asking me whether I want it. I pay him and leave, feeling as if I'm part of something that never gets old and never fails to include me personally.

♭   ♩

My friend Bryan—seller extraordinaire and award-winning vintner—is also a music collector. In fact, when he comes to town, sometimes I'm not sure whether he's visiting me and Carrie or Village Music and John.

During his last visit, we were talking about music, and, as usual, the name of John Goddard came up. While listening to *Miles Davis & John Coltrane Live in Stockholm*—which he was feeling very lucky about finding—he said, "You know, it's hard to think about John without thinking about Village Music at the same time, or Village Music without also thinking about John. It's an artistic association . . . something like trying to think about Trane or Davis without hearing the music. And that's what Village Music is."

"What's that?"

"It's a composition by John, like a painting that he painted himself into and left room for anybody else that wanted to be part of it. And because he's such a bloody genius at it, everyone who sets foot in the store wants to be part of it."

"And then wants to come back," I added.

"Sure. What he has created there—call it whatever fancy marketing name you want to—it's an amalgam of people, product, and feelings that has no formula. You come away with a piece of the store, and you're already thinking about going back for more."

"That's the way it should be."

Music is your own experience, your thoughts, your wisdom. If you don't live it, it won't come out of your horn.

—Charlie Parker

❧15❧

Lesson of the Empty House

Most of us know what's right and wrong without checking statutes or asking the people downtown. You know how you feel when you do something good because you know how you feel when you do something underhanded or behind someone's back. You know when you've told the truth because you know when you haven't. You can answer the big questions without entering a courtroom or boardroom because most of the time you *know* what you're doing. It's not a question of ethics; it's simply you being honest with yourself and other people.

It is that innate honesty that serves as the bedrock of any relationship, be it personal or business.

Ꭾ Ꭿ

It had been more than thirty years since a new house was built in Victor's neighborhood. All the homes occupied an acre or more of forested land, situated on a coastal ridge that afforded each resident uncommon privacy as well as an extraordinary view.

So it wasn't surprising that the neighbors were quite concerned when a longtime resident decided to sell off a piece of his land. They became even more concerned when they learned the parcel was being bought by a contractor who planned to build a spec house.

Rumors raced around the small neighborhood. Some people said they heard the new house was going to be gargantuan, far too large for the site. Others said they heard the contractor had a shaky financial record. One neighbor worried that the new house would look directly into his bedroom window. Families with young children worried about trucks and construction vehicles moving up and down the street where their children played. And everyone worried about the traffic, the inconvenience, and the noise. Especially the noise.

Petitions protesting the sale of the property were circulated. One of the neighbors, particularly outspoken with his objections, volunteered to take the petition to the homeowner and try to convince him not to sell. That's when they learned just how bad the situation was: The neighbor was planning to sell his own house and move out of the country. The neighborhood concerns no longer concerned him, he said. Sorry. Goodbye.

Now angry and more frustrated than ever, a group from the neighborhood asked for a land-use hearing at city hall, but even an ecologically sensitive city council could not keep the homeowner from selling his property.

Construction—or rather, destruction—soon began. Tall redwood trees, some more than three feet in diameter, were cut to the ground. For a while the property looked like a ramshackle logging camp. Victor said that when he first saw the fallen trees being sliced up for garden decorations, he literally became nauseated. It was like watching a rape take place, in full public view, with no one to stop it.

Supporting posts and pillars nearly as long as the fallen trees were erected with the help of cranes and heavy equipment and driven deep into the rich soil. Beams were cantilevered, and an infrastructure was put into place. Neighbors frowned as they passed the site; the contractor and his workers glared back.

Then, a month after construction had begun, all work came to a sudden halt. The word was that the contractor had gone bankrupt and disappeared, leaving the bank holding the bag.

The portable toilet at the construction site was moved, and the city eventually cleared away a tall pile of lumber scraps and other debris. Whenever they walked past the skeletal structure, most people looked straight ahead.

Six months later, the bank sold the partially built house to another developer. When finished, the house was indeed gargantuan: a five-story structure that clung to the steep hillside with four balconies featuring unobscured views and lots of white metal railings. Only the garage and entryway were visible from the street. Victor described it as a contemporary, pugnacious design that seemed to suit no one's fancy except the architect's.

Pugnacious or not, the house was soon sold. Almost no one ever saw or talked to the new resident. People just saw the car, a new black Porsche, parked in the driveway. It was almost as if no one lived there. The neighbors breathed a big

sigh of relief; their fears about loud parties and new distur-
bances were groundless.

Four months later, all the newspapers carried a front-
page story about an investment counselor who was wanted
in connection with a federal fraud investigation. He had si-
phoned off millions of dollars belonging to his clients, including the life savings of many elderly people. He owned
expensive cars, a stable of racehorses, and several homes—
including the new one in Victor's neighborhood.

The newspaper story listed the suspect's address. Now
the neighbors finally knew who their new neighbor was, but
of course he was gone. The papers said he had disappeared
into thin air.

For the next few days, a couple of unmarked FBI cars
sat in the driveway, and soon after that they left. Once again,
the house was vacant, more of a controversy than a dwelling.

ၣ   ၣ

When Victor told me the story of the house, I waited for his
usual commentary, that bit of Victor wisdom that would put
it all in perspective. But Victor was quiet. After a few minutes
I asked him, hesitantly, what this added up to in his mind.

He said, "Let's go for a walk."

"Are we going far?" I asked, reaching for my jacket.

"Not far, just up the street," he said, putting on his
wide-brimmed fedora and adjusting the brim at exactly the
right angle. "I'll show you the house."

As we began walking, he asked me, "What did the
neighbor who originally owned the property do?"

"He sold it without talking to the neighbors."

"What about the contractor who first bought the property?"

"As they say, he bit off more than he could chew."

"And the neighbors, what had they been doing all this time?"

"Signing petitions and getting upset."

We stopped as a doe and her two fawns crossed the road.

"What about the bank?" Victor continued. "What did the bank do?"

"For the neighbors?"

"For anybody."

"Nothing, really. They unloaded the house on another developer."

"What did he do?"

"He finished the house."

Victor kicked a pine cone gently to the side of the road. "How did the neighbors feel about that?"

"They were glad to see it finished."

"Why?"

"Because it was half-finished," I said, a bit snappishly. I felt like I was going around in circles, and my annoyance showed in my voice.

"Why?" he asked again.

"Victor, *why* are you asking me questions I've already answered?"

"Because I don't want the obvious answers. I don't even want an answer at all. Don't think about the *answer*; think about the *question*."

In the deep shade of the redwoods, the light breeze was chilly. I walked with my head down and arms folded. When we rounded the curve, Victor stopped and pointed at the house, a hundred yards ahead. Two blank windows peered at us. The house looked empty and temporary, like a well-constructed shadow.

"Why was that house half-finished?" Victor asked.

"Because no one bought it."

"Stan," Victor asked in a voice that was close to a whisper, "why would anybody buy a half-finished house?"

And suddenly I saw what Victor had been trying to get me to understand. I answered in the same soft tone, speaking very slowly and carefully so as not to disturb the clear vision.

"Of course. The whole house, the whole idea of the house, had never been sold."

"There it is," said Victor with a smile. I'm not sure whether he was referring to the house or to my answer; in any case, we turned away from the empty house and headed home.

As we walked back toward Victor's house, neither of us spoke. That was all right with me: I knew it was one thing to talk and another thing to understand.

My mind was filled with thoughts of the empty house, so new, so troubled, so full of questions. That house was all about something that never happened, something called selling. There had been no presentation, no enthusiasm, no professional pride, no mutual understanding, no communication. There was no sense of a real relationship happening anywhere along the way. The house stood as a lesson of what happens when the objective is profit at any cost, when a sale transaction is nothing more than the signing of papers, and when "out of sight, out of mind" seems to make sense.

After an hour or so of good cognac and good conversation, Victor and I said goodnight. On my way home, I drove around the block for another look at the empty house. It still looked empty, but no longer foreboding. More than anything else, it seemed sad. Feeling grateful, I smiled a farewell. Because of everything it was not, the house had showed me what selling is.

It is better to ask some of the questions than to know all the answers.

— James Thurber

ᕲ16ᕲ

You Communicate
More Than You Know

If I were to ask you what you communicated today, you would probably describe the things you said or wrote, for words are the most obvious components of communication.

You might tell me what a customer said when you asked him to buy your product. You might shake your head and roll your eyes as you relate his skepticism and then nod your head, smile, and gesture expansively when explaining how you answered your customer's objection.

Your gestures and expressions would encourage me to listen to you and help me understand what you said. I would shake my head when you shook your head and smile when you smiled. While you verbally described your communications, we would be communicating nonverbally.

How you say things and how you look may be less obvious components of communication, but it is because of these expressions that your words are heard. Words by themselves account for only a very small portion of your total communication potential. Some experts have estimated it as low as seven percent. The remaining ninety-three percent is *how* you say what you say and how you *look* while you're saying it.

Someone once told me: "You cannot *not* communicate; you are always communicating." When you are thoroughly *you*, you communicate more than you know. You paint these marvelous compositions and place yourself in the foreground by whispering, yelling, mumbling, glaring, smiling, crying, laughing, waving your hands, running, walking, standing up to tell a story or sitting down to listen to one.

There are those times when your words and expressions are marvelously appropriate. You're not sure whether you're doing the listening or the talking, nor does it matter. You're expressing yourself fully and creating a rapport with everyone around you. When you consistently maintain this level of communication, you have the ability to make other people feel good about themselves, which means they feel good about you.

Your most meaningful communications have little to do with words and almost everything to do with feelings. The content of any message is of course important, but it is of little consequence unless it is delivered by the *right person* in the *right way* at the *right time*. Some people call that communicating; other people call it selling.

ꠇ   ꠇ

Along with half a dozen other tired travelers, I watched the baggage carousel without really expecting to see anything new. The same six bags and two cardboard boxes had gone around at least a dozen times. When the conveyor belt and carousel stopped moving, we realized that nothing more was going to show up.

We looked at each other for moral support without finding it. People lifted their eyebrows, rolled their eyes, and shook their heads. Somebody next to me muttered a couple of obscenities, and the person on the other side of me replied, "You can say that again."

I turned around and headed toward the baggage service office in the far corner of the terminal. There was a line —of course. I had spent the day waiting in lines, on freeways and sidewalks, at ticket counters and hot dog stands. Traveling was a long dull lesson in waiting.

At the front of the line, loud voices got louder. A frustrated passenger slammed his hand down on the counter and stormed off, pushing past me through the doorway.

As the line move forward a notch, I heard a child somewhere up in front of me ask, "Why was that man mad, Mommy? Are you mad?" I didn't hear a reply.

The woman behind the counter raised her voice and asked: "Do we have anyone here that reads Spanish? We have a passenger who needs to fill out his application and doesn't read English. Does anyone here speak Spanish?"

Behind me a man replied softly, "*Si.*" He smiled and said, "*Por favor, señor,*" as he stepped ahead of me and went to the counter.

Again I heard the child's voice. "Who is that man, Mommy?" The mother said, "Shhh."

The two Spanish-speaking men stood close together at the counter, quietly conferring about the application form.

We were applying for our lost luggage, which didn't make sense to me. I decided I would not personally fill out an application for *my* property, which *they* had lost.

"Okay, sir, could you move to this end of the counter, please?" The woman gestured to me. Another baggage agent had appeared on the scene, and they were now dividing up the line. The agent said, "Okay, we've had a delay. . . ."

"What do you mean, delay?" I asked.

"Well, it appears that several passengers' baggage was left on the ground at point of departure," she replied, chewing her lip nervously, her eyes on her monitor screen and fingertips tapping the edge of the keyboard. Without looking up, she picked up an application. "Okay, if you'll just fill this out, we'll get you started." When I didn't take the application from her, she looked up and asked impatiently, "Do you have a question?"

"No. I just don't see why I have to do this." It was not one of my finer moments.

She laid the application down on the counter and said in an aggrieved tone, "Sir, your baggage has been misplaced. *And* we are doing everything possible to expedite its return. You can either wait for it here *or* we will have it delivered to your final destination before 8 A.M. tomorrow morning, *but* in order to do that, *you* must fill out this information so that we will know *which* baggage is yours and how you would like us to handle it."

I had a brilliant rejoinder on the tip of my tongue, but just then I heard the child's voice again. In my haste to reach the counter, I hadn't noticed the people around me. I turned and saw a harried young mother holding a little girl in white pajamas, probably no more than three years old. Raising herself halfway up out of her mother's arms, she asked the baggage agent: "Can you bring Bear back?"

The little girl looked straight into the eyes of the baggage agent, her blue eyes serious and troubled. She was not smiling, she was not glaring. She was just looking at another human being with everything that she was about. She totally consumed the moment, and I knew no one was going to say a thing until that agent answered that question.

The agent rested her fingers on the keyboard and looked at the little girl for a matter of moments. Then she smiled and said with true conviction: "I'll bring Bear back, sweetheart."

When she smiled at the little girl, the agent was transformed into a person doing something for another person rather than just an overstressed official doing a job. She turned to me and, picking up the application lying on the counter, said, "Here, let me fill this out for you. It'll probably go faster that way."

As I gave her all the pertinent information, I realized that the steamy little office had immediately become more spacious, and everyone in it had become more relaxed. A small child, and a meaningful communication, had broken through our collective foul mood. Before leaving, I smiled at the little girl and said, "Thank you."

℘　ℐ

Victor called the next day to ask about my trip. I told him about a project that I had finalized, told him what airline not to fly, and then I told him about a little girl whose expression and sense of purpose had held the emotions of several adults hostage for a few moments.

"That's a good story," Victor said, "Tell it to me again when I see you."

"Why?"

"Because we're talking on the telephone. Remember what Durrell said about telephones." He was right. I could see the receiver in my hand, but I couldn't see Victor. The telephone was a better-than-nothing device for better-than-nothing communications. I recalled the Lawrence Durrell quotation to which Victor had referred: "The telephone is the symbol of communications that never take place."

Then I remembered the communication that recently had taken place in the baggage office. It wasn't what she had said, it was how she had said it—*as if it were the only thing worth saying at that moment*. It was a lesson I would always remember.

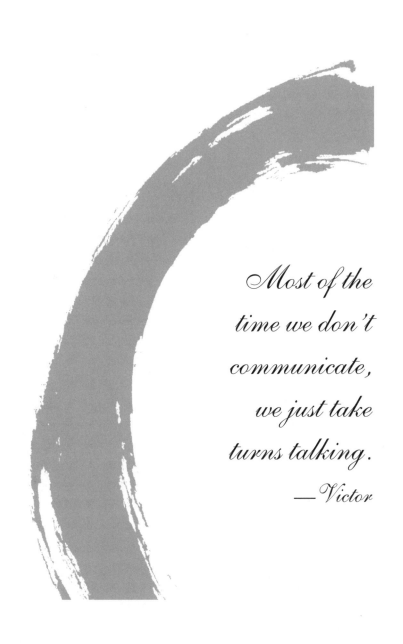

*Most of the
time we don't
communicate,
we just take
turns talking.*
—*Victor*

❧17❧

Addressing Yourself

When I was a teenager rebelling against everything that smacked of authority or bounds, I spent a lot of time with my best friend, Dan. I think I had a crush on his mother, Eleanor, and I paid close attention to everything she did. One afternoon, as Dan and I were leaving to attend a jazz concert in Los Angeles, she hugged us both and said, "Take care." I'm sure she thought of it as nothing special, but that gentle farewell made me stop and think.

Yes, I thought, that's a good thing to say. There was something worldly, sophisticated about those words. It wasn't something I could hear a kid saying—which meant that I started using it right away.

Those two simple words of goodbye spoke worlds about symmetry and balance. I knew that if I was to take care, it meant watching out for more than myself, the person doing the walking. It also meant caring for the things that I walked past, choosing my steps carefully and taking a softer stride. More than watching where *I* was going, it cautioned me to watch where other people were going as well.

Since then, I have used that farewell thousands of

times. I find that when I'm talking with a young salesperson just getting started, I say it with a special resonance. Looking at that bright face, full of excitement and energy, eager for the next thing to *do*, I remember how that all feels, and part of me wants to add, "Wait. Go steady." I feel myself wanting to say something about balance.

As a salesperson, it is your job to inspire people to do things that they have only thought about. You work hard to turn fantasies into realities. You often have to assure people that they will be satisfied because *you* will make it right. It is your business and your responsibility to give people a sense of fun and fulfillment. You initiate lifelong relationships with your customers and influence their lifestyles much like a teacher giving guidance to pupils.

The better you are at your job, the more responsibiltiy you take on and the more profound your impact on your customers' lives. However, if things do not go according to plan or if unavoidable circumstances intervene, then fun and fulfillment can turn to confusion and disappointment for both yourself and your customer. There is that possibility with every sale.

The dynamics of selling, the good and the bad together, can weight heavily upon you. If you do not *take care* and maintain a sense of personal balance, you can be overpowered by the stress of it all. You must find a place for the things that are meaningful to you beyond the business of selling.

Every sales professional eventually realizes there are ways to find peace of mind other than making a sale. Whether it be a walk or a run through the park, listening to music, reading a book, being by yourself, or spending time with someone you love—it should be a regular pursuit. And often it is something to pursue, for sometimes the things that will do us the most good are the most elusive.

Take care to have the time of your life, and be as responsible for your own well-being as for that of your customers; remember, if you lose your balance, it is difficult to guide someone else.

ᖷ   ᖩ

A couple of years ago, a dear friend of Carrie's was going through a difficult time. Carrie has a tendency to sometimes step over the line that separates empathy from sympathy and become more involved that she had originally intended. She carried her friend's troubles on her own shoulders and as a result was becoming very depressed.

Victor, visiting one evening, noticed her somber mood and inquired. Carrie told him a little of what was happening, adding that maybe she needed to think more about personal balance—"whatever that term really means," she added.

"With your permission, Carrie, I'd like to tell you a story about personal balance. Have I ever told you much about my oldest son, John?"

Of course he hadn't, for Victor rarely talked about his family. There were some things that he seldom discussed because he considered them precious, so we were flattered and at the same time intrigued.

John had been the kid who was supposed to get a medical degree. But, after attending five or six universities, mostly on a part-time basis, he emerged from academia with a bachelor's degree in language arts, which had very little to do with how he would spend his life.

John, now forty-eight years old, had started traveling at the age of sixteen, when most kids were just getting their driver's license. He made his way to strange, exotic, and sometimes dangerous places. He called himself a journalist because he wrote about his seemingly aimless travels in journals. It was the journals more than the traveling that became his discipline and his greatest pleasure.

His travels were usually inspired by people he knew and loved.

A girlfriend who had made her way past the government authorities into the rain forests at the bottom of Mexico wrote and told him about an ancient Mayan ruin she had discovered buried under the jungle. She had more than scratched the surface and discovered glyphs that had not been seen for centuries. "Come quickly," she wrote, and John immediately packed his bags and flew off to Chiapas as if the structures that had withstood three thousand years of weathering and erosion were going to disintegrate unless he got there the next week.

A good friend wrote to John from Algiers. He was living in an inn that had once sheltered the likes of Paul and Jane Bowles, William Burroughs, Jean-Paul Sartre, Simone de Beauvoir, and others. The landlord had been friends with all of them, and he had amazing stories to tell. "Come quickly," the friend wrote, and John boarded a plane to Algiers as casually as someone else would take a bus across town.

Another girlfriend called him from Woolongong, Aus-

tralia. She had found the house that D. H. Lawrence had
lived in while writing *Kangaroo*. The little plaque out front
was hidden by a kiwi bush loaded with fruit that you could
eat, skin and all. She was thrilled and knew he would be too.
John was on the other side of the world the next day. Victor
still had a little ruddy stone in his library that John had
brought to him straight from D. H. Lawrence's front yard.

Most people had a home base and traveled for vaca-
tions, but John seemed to be more at home traveling and
thought of his sojourns at home as vacation. He traveled as
if the world were his backyard and the seven seas just so
many puddles beside the pathway.

Victor traveled a great deal himself, of course, and
sometimes his trajectory would intersect with John's. Victor
would arrive at a hotel in Paris, and there would be a post-
card from his son with a new return address. Through the
years they carried on a regular, and fascinating, correspondence. One of the most fascinating things about it was how
the letters and postcards ever managed to find their respec-
tive destinations.

One year, Victor told us, he took a limousine from the
airport in Mexico City to the Del Prado Hotel, where a special suite had been reserved for him. While the desk clerk
was checking him in, the manager came out of the back office and greeted him warmly. "And I mustn't forget to give
you this," he said, handing Victor a nine- by twelve-inch
manila envelope posted in Thailand.

Victor waited until he got to his room and arranged his
things before opening the envelope. Inside he found thirteen
sealed letters, all identical except for one. Inscribed on it was

the simple message: "Open immediately." Victor opened the letter *immediately*, not bothering to look at the others.

This letter was different from any other John had ever written. It was forthright and intimate, absent of philosophical ruminations, speaking directly to Victor, almost as if his son were in the same room with him.

Without much preface, John wrote that Clea, the girl whom he had joined in the jungles of Mexico and whom he had been in love with most of his young life, had had a dreadful accident, and things did not look good. Victor immediately checked the postmark, but it was smeared and illegible, and the letter, as usual, was not dated. John dated only what he wrote in his journals.

John went on to say that he knew he was too far away to get to her in time, so instead he was going the opposite way. To the mountains, he said, the "land of snows." He was not running away from anything; instead, he was going away to find something. He said not to expect any correspondence anytime too soon. There were things he must do, but he needed a little bit of help and a lot of intuition.

He went on to explain that the other letters were not for Victor to read, but for Victor to send. Victor looked at the other letters. Each one carried Victor's U.S. return address, and each one was self-addressed to John in care of a hotel in Lhasa, Tibet.

In his letter, John said that the one really worthwhile thing that he had done during the course of his travels was to keep track of himself in his journals. He wrote about things that made him feel good, bad, or better; things that made him think more clearly; things that shook him out of complacency; things that made him feel like loving others and himself as much as he should. He said it was something like a "mind-body tool kit." He half-apologized for the cuteness of it all, but he said that his main project all of his life had been himself. Learning how to live happily with himself and others had always been his objective, and it still was.

In his letter, he cited some examples of things he had cataloged. Items such as "watch a sunset and sip tea; draw pictures in the sand for seagulls to ponder; take a walk without knowing where you're going; write about something you don't want to write about; eat ice cream; remember what holidays at home felt like; hug the first person you see whom you know (make sure you know them); write a letter to the person who's been on your mind today; think about the last person you talked to in the last place you visited (for people are the real markers on the compass); sit without thinking until your body feels like one big strained muscle, then relax, falling weightless, forever."

John explained that he had spent the past forty-eight hours in an unexpectedly clear state of mind. He had not slept; maybe he had catnapped, but always he awoke with the pen in his hand and another journal entry on his mind. Without consciously organizing them, he had sorted out the items, and they became the body of future letters—twelve letters in all.

The instructions were very simple: Whenever Victor felt like it—"felt" as only a person who loves another can feel—he was to send a letter *from* John *to* John. And if he felt like dropping a line of his own, it would be appreciated.

Victor was to take his time sending the letters, John said, because he would be in the vicinity of this address for a long while. He wanted to walk the narrow paths of Samye Chimpu where Guru Rinpoche, "Precious Teacher," had walked. He wanted to see prayer flags flapping in the wind fourteen thousand feet up in the air. He wanted to go where a pilgrim must finally go, for he was just that, a simple pilgrim.

In Victor's letter he wrote, "I think I understand about Clea, and that's very good because she never sought to be a source of confusion for anyone in her entire life."

Victor told Carrie and me that it was one of the most intimate and revealing times that he had ever spent with his son. Sitting there on the end of a bed in a hotel in Mexico City with tears in his eyes, hearing the laughter of his son in his mind as he read John's last line: "So until I hear from you, or me, the next time, I love you, Dad. Yours truly, John."

Victor looked at us both without saying anything for a few moments, then added, "That letter taught me more about my life and my son than any letter I was ever privileged to receive.

"And Carrie"—he bent forward, touching her gently on the shoulder—"John is well, and all because he made something they now call 'personal balance' the center of his life. As he said, he was his own project, much as all of us should be. Carrie, maybe you should write yourself a letter, or two, and pass them on to someone to send to you someday. Sometimes you can tell yourself things that no one else can even begin to tell you, simply because we all know ourselves much better than we usually like to admit.

"John still lives in Tibet, and I've visited him a couple of times. The last time was an extended stay, and I have no illusions about his being anywhere else. He no longer writes in his journals. He said he ran out of paper, but I think there might be another explanation."

ၣ   ၣ

I remember taking a letter from my desk, one of those that Carrie had addressed to herself, and thinking, should I send this now or should I send it some other time? I wondered what Victor would have done. When was the right time to send a person her own best advice?

I shook my head, feeling foolish. There I was, wanting to help someone whom I loved deeply, and I had something in my hand that might help, and I was asking myself should I wait until some other time. I remembered Victor telling me: "When you feel like doing something for someone, please do." I went to the closest mailbox and mailed the letter.

The next night, Carrie had a smile on her face. "I got this wonderful letter today."

"Oh?"

"Yes, it was the last of the letters I wrote to myself. And, it's very strange, but I think I'm going to miss them," she said, her eyes sparkling as she smiled at me.

"Maybe that's the way it is when you run out of paper."

But go on loving
what is good, simple
and ordinary;
animals and things
and flowers, and keep
the balance true.

—Rainer Maria Rilke

Farewell

Take your heart, your skills, your love of what you're doing, and make them work for you and the people you serve, who are called customers. Make them proud that you were the person they were fortunate enough to meet.

Of all the things you do in life, nothing is so true as what you do for others. Selling is your opportunity to touch people beyond your reach and to be more than an average professional on an uphill swing.

The sales will always come your way, but be aware that you must work hard for the relationships. Whatever you accomplish that is worth remembering is always on behalf of someone else.

This means good business, personally and professionally. And that is your goal—to live mindfully, with spirit and energy, expressing joy in the name of something called selling. Make it as worthwhile for someone else as for yourself. Give and take as you would a precious gift.

When your eyes greet those of the customer as surely as light in a reflection, and when smiles pass between you like a gentle breeze, then you know you are where you should be and want to be, and never will you, the seller, be happier.

As for the book, **the Zen of selling,** *my name is on the cover, but the book is truly yours. Use it, have fun with it, and reread your favorite stories to yourself and your friends.*
    Take care.

—*Stan*